For Whom the Bell Tolls

HATJE CANTZ

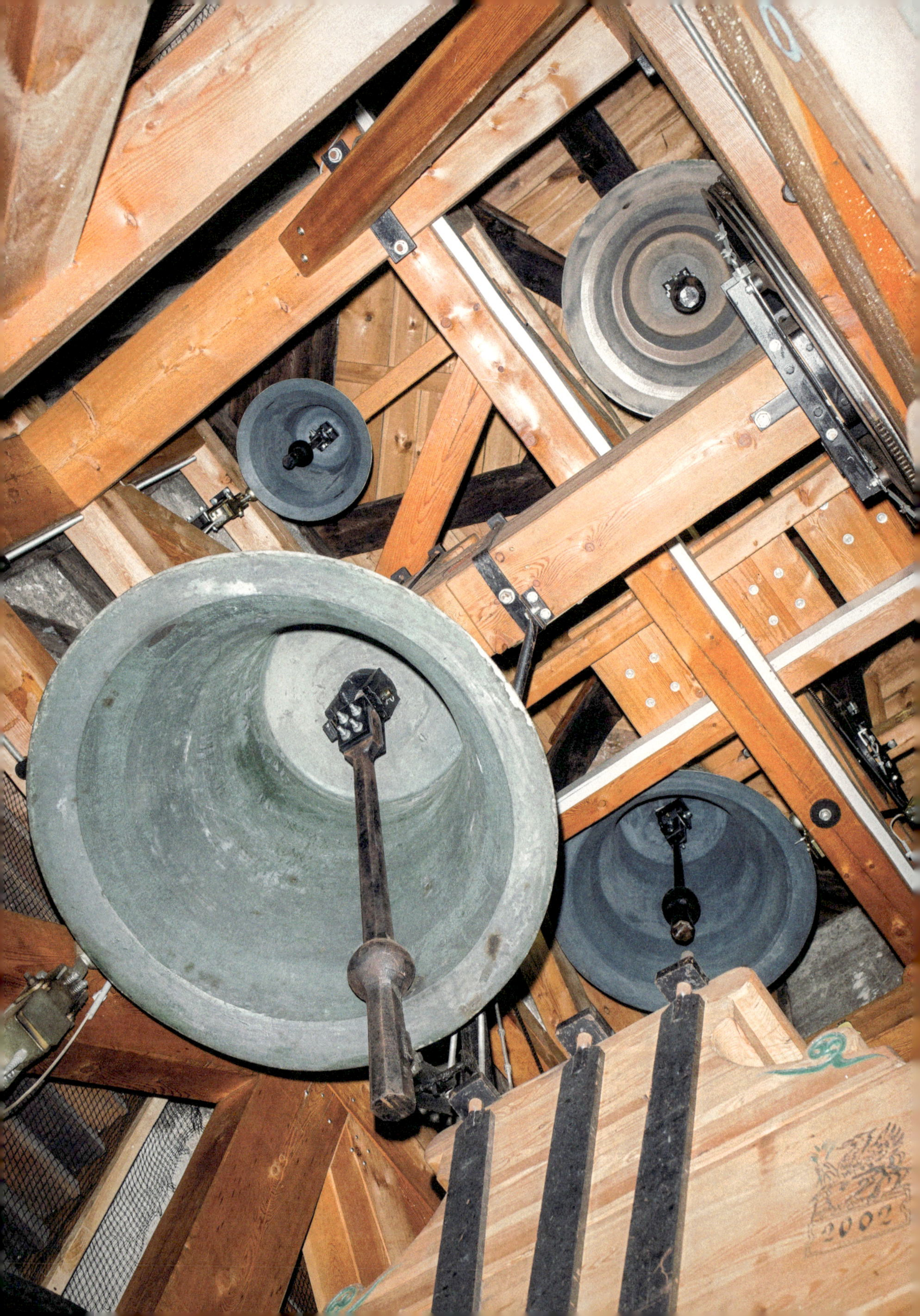

Contents

Introduction by
M a r c   S p i e g l e r

I still remember, quite distinctly, walking into a.m. space's booth in the Discoveries section during the 2015 Art Basel show in Hong Kong. Even amidst the hubbub of an art fair, something convinced me to slow my pace and dive into Samson Young's installation. Perhaps it was the artist himself, drumming pensively, or the naval maps and radio gear arrayed around him. The gestalt felt fully formed—not the experimental jabs or suggestive-yet-insubstantial gestures typical of young artists, but rather a microcosm drawn from a much larger world inside Samson's head.

Fortunately for Samson, and for us, the BMW Art Journey jury felt the same way. Looking backward over the eighteen months that have passed since then, it is hard to imagine how this story could have unrolled more perfectly.

First of all—the sine qua non—Samson's project, *For Whom the Bell Tolls,* has the intellectual rigor and aesthetic innovation that mark a breakthrough piece. And its global scope fits seamlessly with the core notion of the award: that even in a digital world—no, especially in a digital world—physical voyages unleash powerful creative forces. The project managed to lyrically comment on humanity's inescapable oscillation between peace and conflict —without seeming didactic or preachy, no easy feat.

Winning the journey did not make Samson Young a fascinating artist. But it broadcast his unique talents to a global audience, with massive ripple effects. In short order, he started working with three premier galleries, on three continents: Gisela Capitain, the legendary Cologne gallerist and Kippenberger confidante; New York's downtown mainstay Team Gallery; and Calcutta's Experimenter Gallery, a force in Southeast Asia. In March 2016, his sonic walking tour of Wan Chai and Admiralty marked a return engagement with Art Basel Hong Kong, the fair that launched him into the global art world. Then, three months later, he unveiled his birdsong performance piece at Unlimited at Art Basel in Switzerland: In a witty yet profound repurposing, Samson used a Long Range Acoustic Device to transect the immense hall with sonic waves, deploying a technology often unleashed by authority forces when suppressing demonstrators to instead create a magical moment.

Samson Young's career has only just begun. We will hear from him for years to come. And his debut BMW Art Journey has set the bar high for all the artists who follow him, by demonstrating the immense potential of this opportunity. This book, evoking the trip that took Samson to discover and document bells worldwide, offers us a window into the creative process of an artist whom we will proudly remember accompanying at such a pivotal phase in his voyage.

Marc Spiegler
is Art Basel's global director.

Foreword by
T h o m a s   G i r s t

Very much aware that any remarks bordering on the hagiographical may sound as embarrassing as they are presumptuous, apt to be of disservice to both reader and artist, I would nonetheless be negligent to fail to admit that during my two decades in the art world, I have never come across anyone more sincere, hilarious, hyperintelligent, modest, passionate, humble, untiring, obsessed, sensitive, and hard-working than Samson Young.

In late August 2015, I had the privilege of traveling in France with Samson for three days, when he was working on *For Whom the Bell Tolls: A Sonic Journey into the History of Conflict*. Local historians in the most remote hamlets of the Auvergne generously invited us to their homes for elaborate dinners and discussions about historic bells that lasted well into the night. Priests opened up ancient churches for us with massive brass keys. Together we climbed high steeples on brittle wooden ladders. A sense of wonderment and adventure suffused those moments, as Samson's meticulous planning was set into motion on those flawless, humid summer days

I remember holding onto the artist's ankles so he could crouch underneath a huge bronze bell to study the letters on its other side. Endeavors such as this were not entirely without danger: The enormous bell went off automatically every fifteen minutes and could have rendered Samson deaf or smashed his shoulders. We were up high in the belfry of l'Église Saint-Hilaire de Brezons, at

Vigouroux, surrounded by blue skies, 18th-century farmhouses, and nothing else but valleys, meadows, and forests in every shade of green. "Don't tell anyone I'm wearing Mickey Mouse socks," he smiled, as I gripped him as firmly as I could. And his smile grew even wider when he finally spotted what he was looking for: an inscription ascribing magic powers to the bell to keep the thunder away as far as it could be heard.

When Samson recorded and visualized the sounds around him, he included those of a dog barking, of hens scratching and clucking, of a pickup truck motoring by. He knew that the omnipresent possibility of failure can be liberating. In spite of this, "an artist must have a robust work ethic," he later told me. "The most important thing is to work, and to create and sustain the circumstances that will allow one to continue to work." I am certain that this work ethic, as well as the sheer depth of his engagement with anything he chooses to focus on, will make Samson Young steer clear of the multitudinous traps the art world lays for those it most reveres.

T h o m a s   G i r s t
is head of cultural engagement at the BMW Group.

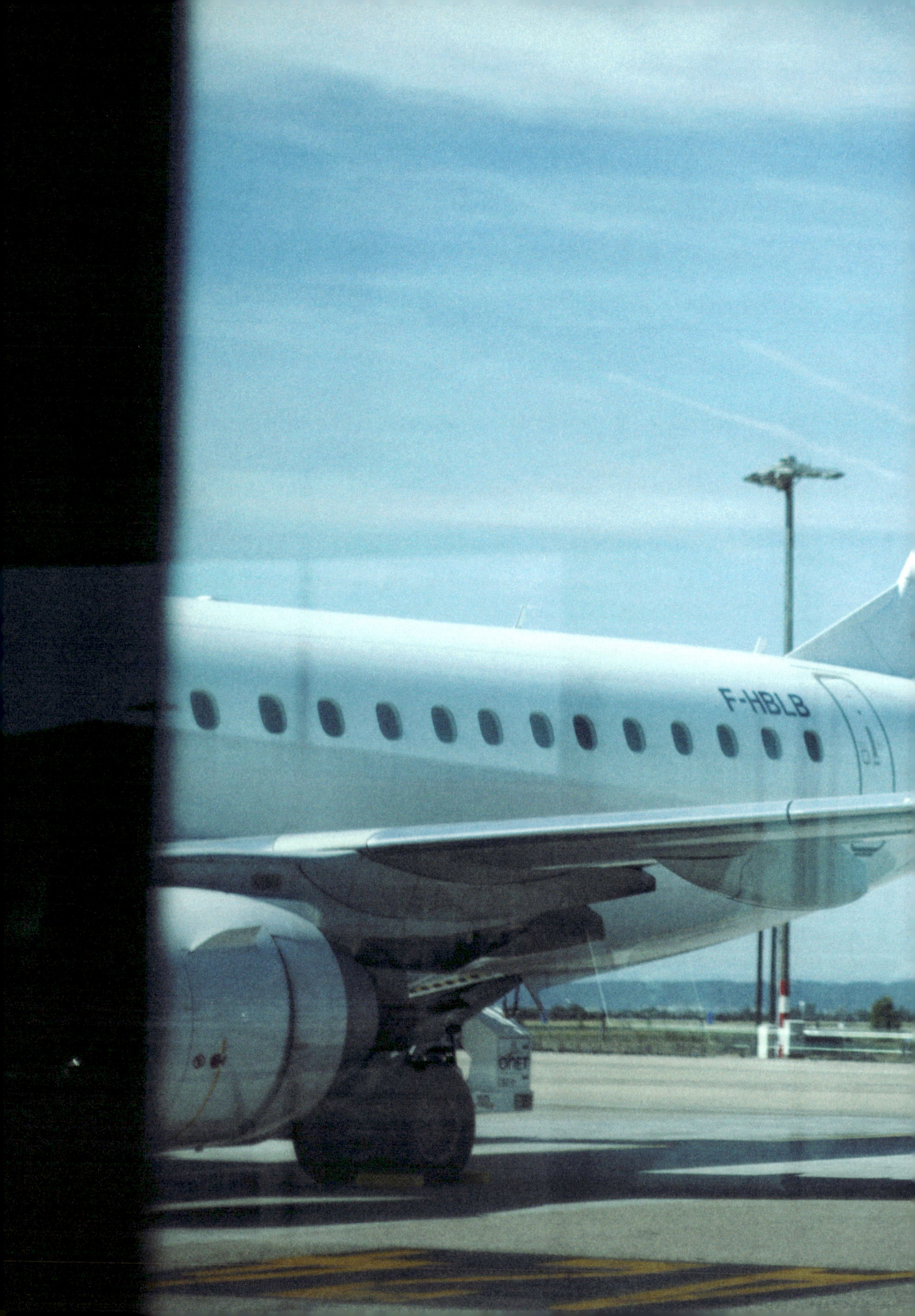

F-HBLB

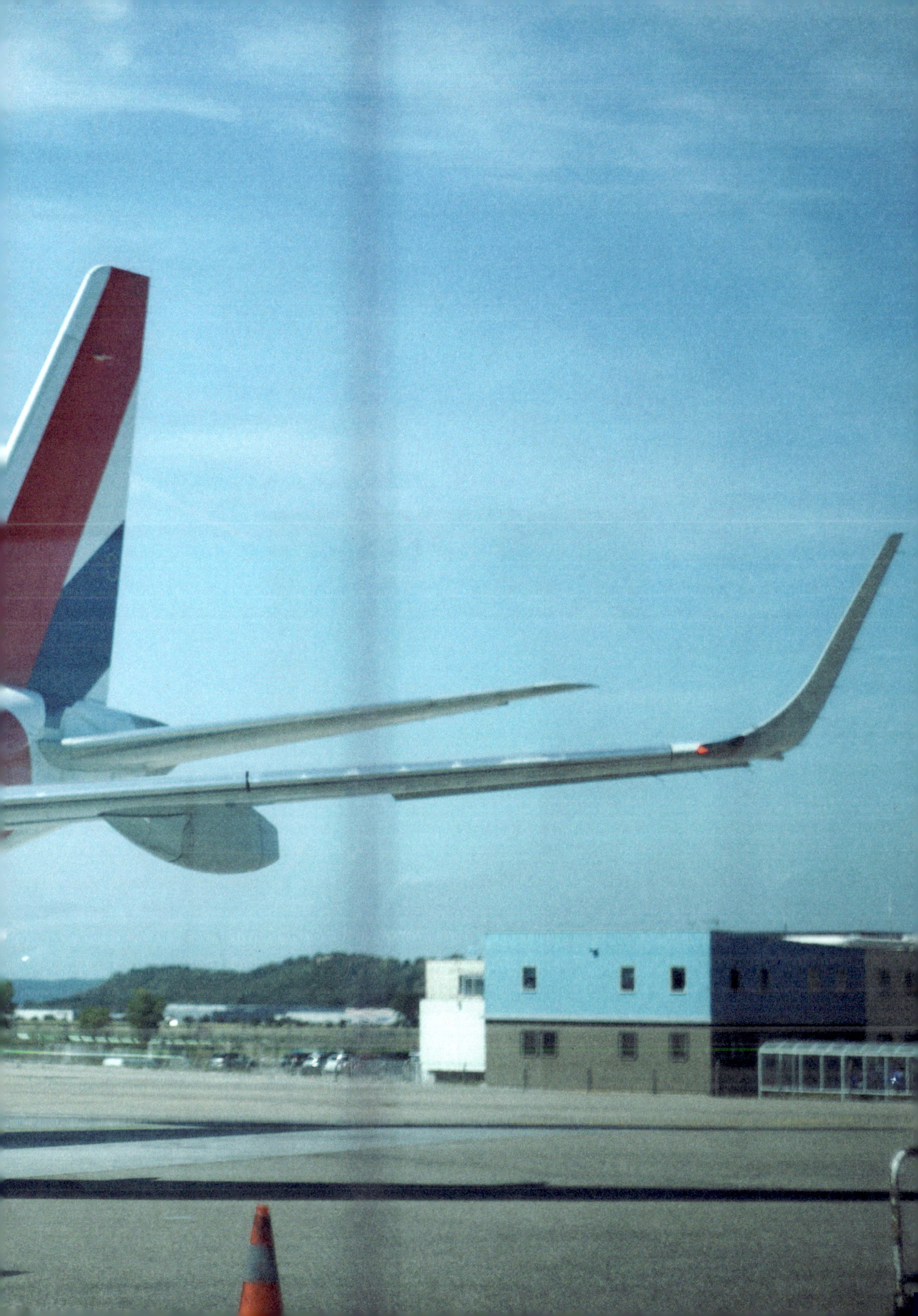

Samson Young in Conversation
with András Szántó

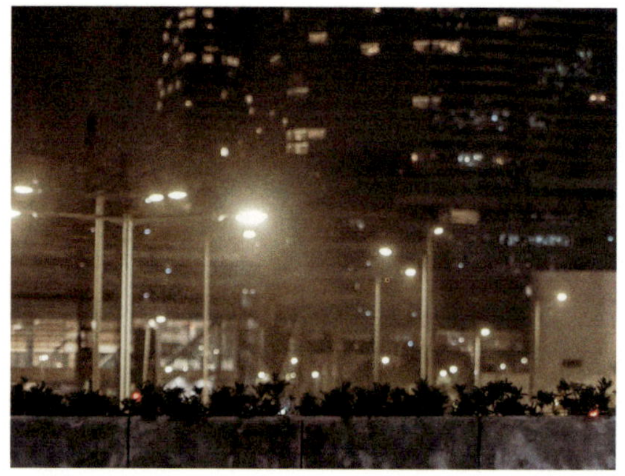

**As we speak, you are just about to set out on the
first phase of your journey, which will take you
to Burma, various European cities, then Morocco,
Kenya, and Australia—all in search of bells.
What is it about bells that fascinates you?**

There are really many things. I actually hit upon the
topic of bells quite naturally following on from my
last project. I was thinking about how, before indus-
trialization, the only man-made items able to make a
sound louder than the sounds of nature would have
been weapons, such as cannons, and bells. Before
the dawn of machines, we had only these two clas-
ses of objects able to make loud noises.

This is common across cultures—it's the same for
Europe, China, Japan, all kinds of places. Each cul-
ture has its own use and form for bells. China has
ritual bells, and of course, bells are very important
in Buddhism. In Europe, bells call to prayer. There
are secular bells used to mark time. And bells also
spread through missionaries and via conquest.
Different cultures have adopted bells for different
purposes. In Buddhist temples, bells are rung in
a certain way, while the British came up with their
own form of bellringing. Despite this diversity, as
a physical object, bells retain a common form.
They all look somewhat similar, and that has to do
with acoustic science. There is a good way to make
a bell draw out the nuance in the object. I find this
very interesting.

**What does a bell, as a metaphor, mean to you
personally?**

For me, a bell creates a kind of "information overload." There are certain sounds that our ears cannot fully comprehend in the moment. An explosion
is another example of that kind of sound. The sound
of a bell is so complex that you can listen to it several
times and each time it means something else to you.
If you get a recording of a bell, put it through the
computer and look at the spectrogram of the sound,
it has so many complex harmonics. Your ear cannot
help but draw information from it while you are listening. You'll hear something different every time.

Which is remarkable, as the sound of a bell lasts for
only a few seconds, but by listening repeatedly, you
discover more. The other interesting thing about
the sound of a bell is that, in your mind, you can de-
lay the reverberation—you imagine it carries on for
longer than it actually does. It is a perfect metaphor
for the fact that something immensely physical is,
in fact, psychological. It is a physical vibration, but
really it is a kind of hallucination if you think about it.

**You are a composer as well as an artist, and the
way you talk about all this is clearly informed by
your professional study of sound and its cultural history. How do these two things connect?**

I don't know whether I am really conscious of that
split creative personality, as it were. What I am interested in is how my musical training structured my
world and allows me to see and hear the world in a
certain way. By being conscious of this, I try to work
against it but also use it as a springboard.

**The duality of the bell as a sound and also an
object is clearly a fascination of yours.**

Bells are such beautiful physical objects that some-
times that's what we focus on. But what my musical
training has given me is this enhanced attention to
the way the sound actually spreads, and how the
sounds that bells produce become this network of
relations. I really think of bells both as stationary
physical objects and something fluid and dynamic
that draws communities in—something that spreads
out and gathers, calling together individuals in a community, just by virtue of the sound being heard in
its vicinity.

**Describe your process when you come in direct
contact with a bell.**

So, for example, when I listen to a bell, I will try to
listen to its color, and I'll listen to the volume. Then
I'll try to translate those qualities into shapes and no-
tations. Some things can only be dealt with in shapes,
such as the color of the sound and the shape of its
reverberation—these cannot be notated accurately;

you have to use your imagination and invent a system. Then with things like the pitch of the sound itself, I can record the sound and feed it through a computer analysis program to look at the pitch content, which I note more accurately.

I also like to break things down into phases. For instance, there is a first phase when the bell rings, then a second when it resonates. So it is a combination of metaphorical and inaccurate shapes, plus metaphorical representation.

How did the project *For Whom the Bell Tolls* take shape in your mind?

The initial point of departure was this idea, this connection between bells and cannons. Then, as I was drafting my proposal for the Art Journey, I started to become very aware of the appropriateness of bells as a way to make a journey, as a point of focus for a journey. As I mentioned before, bells cross cultures and history. They have a long history across many religions and are mentioned a lot in literature.

There are numerous references to bells in poetry and works of fiction, which I also refer to on this journey. And the sound of bells, of course, has a history in music, spanning Western classical orchestral music to ancient court music in China.

So it really gives me this incredible opportunity to go from fiction to reality, history to current affairs.

When I was thinking of travel, I wasn't just thinking of travel to distant places, but of traveling, really, in time, through stories and ideologies.

Then I had to narrow down the topic somewhat. What I have been focusing on over the past few years has been the idea of conflict. So I started with one thing that blew up into this huge project, almost too big to manage, which I then narrowed down into one personal fascination that I have been working with.

Where will this journey lead?

A lot of the bells are in places outside of Asia. I did this deliberately because I wanted to take advantage of this opportunity to go to places which would not otherwise be accessible to me—either because it would be too costly or because the bells are in collections hard for individual artists to negotiate access to. After this art journey, I will be in a position to see bells in China myself. This process is just the beginning. I will probably work on this for years and years. The bells have to do with conflict and they have to be far away or inaccessible—these are the criteria that shape my choices.

Give me some examples of an iconic bell that you plan to investigate, and the complexity and meanings surrounding it?

The focus of this project is to think about "for whom these bells toll." In Australia, I found a bell in Darlington Point, a very small town in New South Wales. In 1880, an English pastor set up a Christian mission there, intended to serve the Aboriginal community as a way of raising their standard of living, and to provide them with necessities and an education. Unlike many other missionaries at that time, who despite their good intentions were actually implicated in a lot of violence and aggression toward the Aboriginal community, this particular pastor—at least according to archival documents—really did a lot to improve the life of the local indigenous people. But then the Australian government of the time forcefully disbanded the mission, as it was thought the mission was encouraging Aboriginal Australians to get together on a regular basis, which the government saw as a threat.

That mission had a bell, which was then put into storage. Afterward, the Australian government moved in and had the children forcibly adopted by white Australians as part of the White Australia policy at the time. The mission bell was reinstalled in another church in Darlington Point—now quite a suburban area—where it remains in use today. So this bell now rings for a very different community, and this is not a history that is mentioned that often.

I got in touch with the reverend of the church, and am going to record the bell and interview the reverend. She is also going to put me in touch with descendants of individuals whose lives were touched by that English pastor. This is in a town located six hours by car from Sydney. It's a good example of the kind of research I can do on this journey.

Your process involves extensive research. Tell me a bit more about how you actually go about analyzing these bells.

I will visit foundries and learn about casting. I have also been learning about bells from Eastern Europe which were stored in Germany after the war and subsequently returned to Eastern Europe. Just today, I received a note from a museum that is home to a bell archive. They have a very extensive record of where bells had been returned to, and their archives also contain fragments of some of the bells that were destroyed. I am hoping they might allow me to do either a cast or a 3D scan of these fragments. I am not yet sure what I will do with them. You can now do 3D scans with your iPad, so I will scan the fragments.

There is another bell in Kenya, the slave-trading bell in Mombasa. I got in touch with the National Museum and they have a cast of this bell, which, again, I hope to scan when I am there. I can produce many different things from 3D scans, but they lend themselves to the production of objects. I am not sure how I will then present it.

One of the things you have in mind for after you complete this journey is to create a musical work with the bell sounds. Can you tell me more about that?

For that project, I want the orchestra to become an extension of the very complex reverberation of these bells. I am going to have all these recordings of bells and produce a multi-channel electronic sound piece with these recordings. But the ring of a bell only lasts for a couple of seconds, so I want the orchestra to draw out the bells' reverberation and decay. It goes back to what I was talking about, the idea of hearing as a form of hallucination.

When you listen to a concert of, say, piano music, at the end of the piece, the musician often holds the last reverberation of sounds, and holds her posture, with the sustaining pedal down. And as long as the pianist holds her posture, you can almost hear that decay going on forever, on and on and on, until she stands up to receive the applause. And that is a beautiful moment, because you can never tell when that musical moment will recede. Your imagination has become engaged. That is very interesting to me, and bells have that same quality. That is what I will seek to capture in this piece. I want to use the orchestra as a canvas to extend the sound. It will probably be quite minimal, but also lush and complex.

Has travel always been part of your artistic practice? What has it meant for you, and what do you think travel brings, in general, to the story of art?

Going to different places for a singular purpose has always been a part of my work. I did a piece earlier where I walked the border between Hong Kong and China. This idea of going to places as a way of collecting material and to complete a line or a system is something I have always been interested in. I see this project as an extension of that. Of course, I have never traveled this far and wide.

Another thing that interests me in terms of travel is that there is always the idea of the traveling landscape artist who goes to different places and does sketches of the landscape. There is a history in that. I was thinking to myself: *What is the equivalent of that for a sound artist?* I guess that is what I am doing: going to different places and producing sketches of the aural landscape. I am sort of sketching the sound of landscape, in a way.

As an Asian artist who trained in the US, how do you expect this journey will change your perception of the world and of your work as an artist?

This is really very important for me as a project—the scale of it is something I have never attempted before. Although it is a big step up for me in terms of size, it is also quite organic. I am extending the themes and concerns I have been working with previously.

This is the most international and the largest-scale project I have ever attempted.

The projects I have worked on before have been very geographically specific. Many of them focused on Hong Kong, or wherever I was living at the time. This is the first where I have taken a more global view. Of course, each location has its own micro-narrative. But the scope is universal. That is something new to me, and I'm really enjoying the challenge. It also allows me to enter into a conversation with the works of many artists who have explored related themes before.

If there were a single overarching question that you were trying to answer through this journey, what would it be?

I want to find out how sound draws people in and draws the world in, and, at the same time, how it manages to keep the world at arm's length. By looking at issues which are common but universally important, I am able to take a stance that is both intimate and has a certain objectivity. That's why I need to look at these issues through sound, and that's what makes my work unique. Now all these ideas can come together.

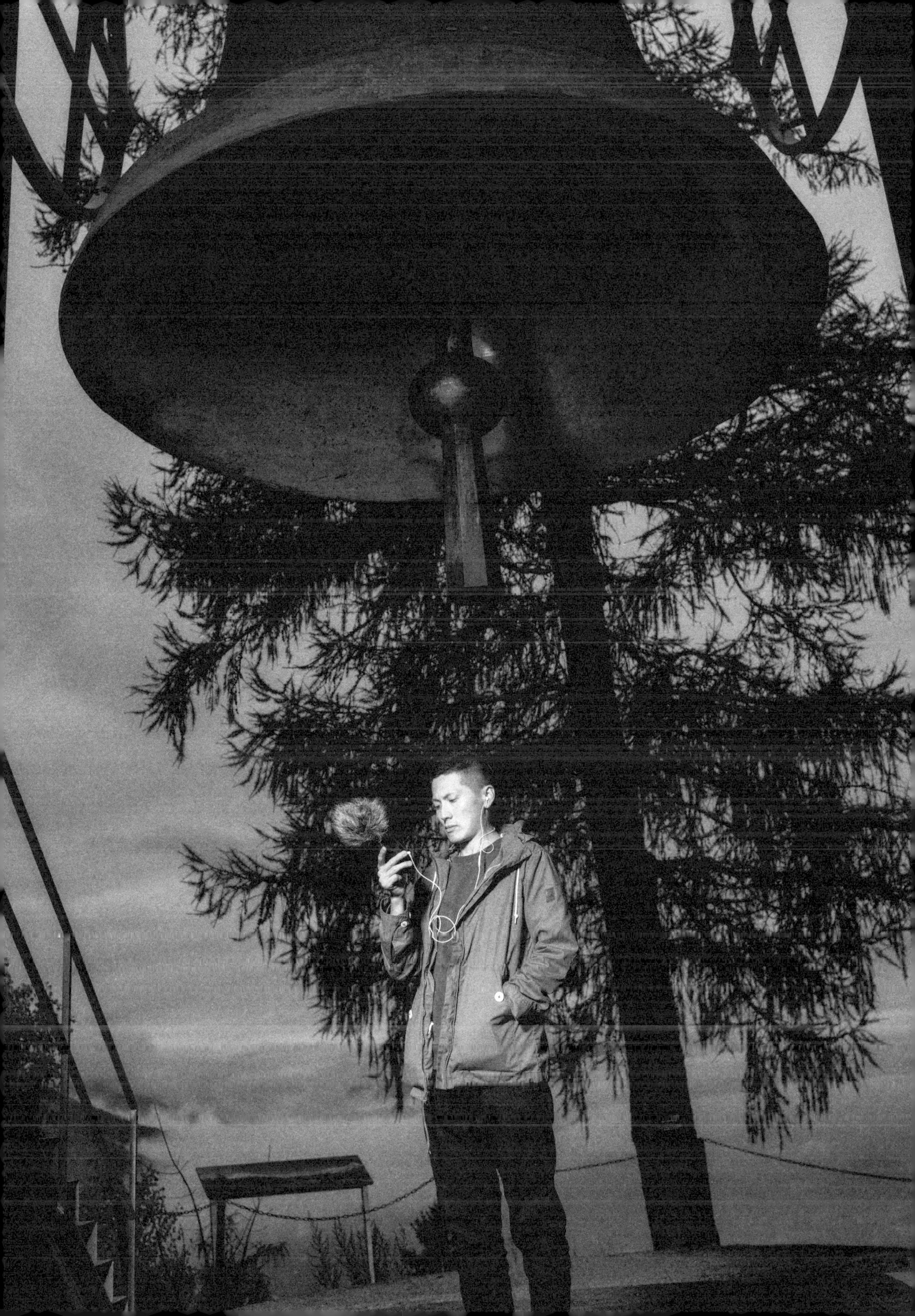

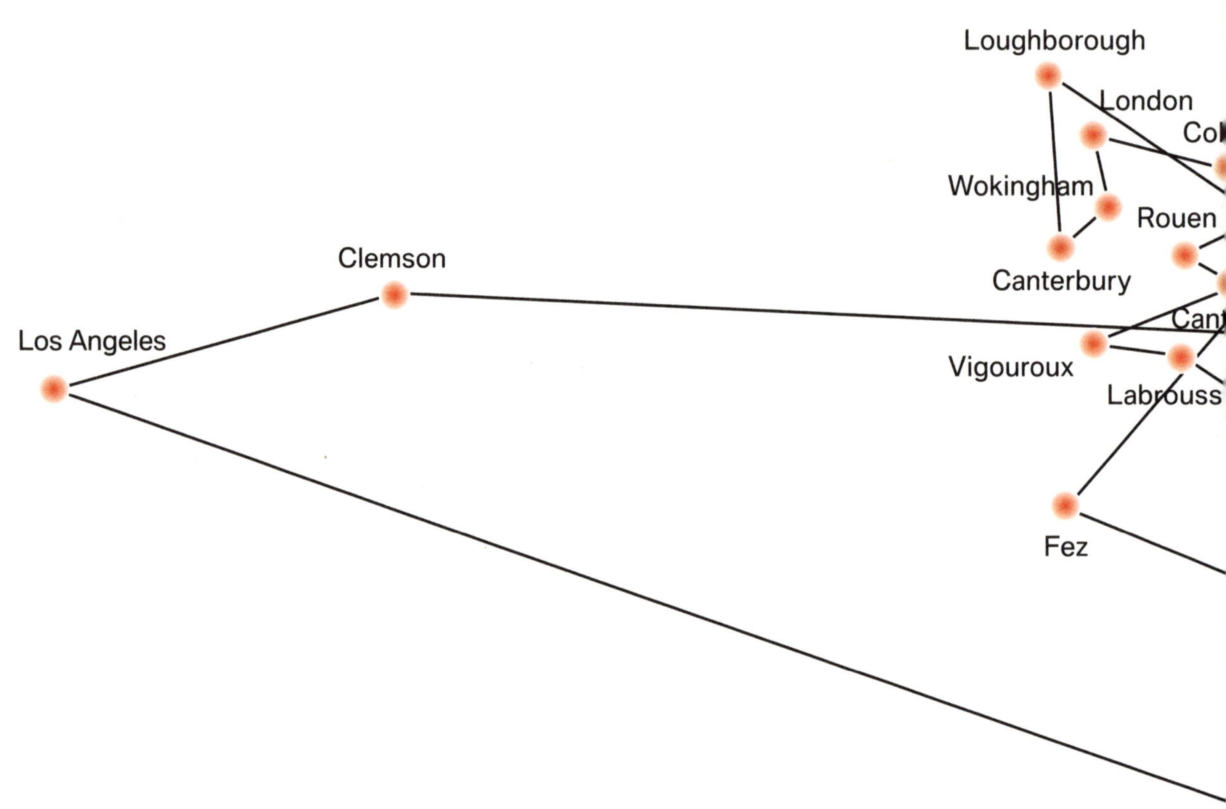

Listen to the Sounds of the Journey

To experience the sounds of bells visited during Samson Young's journey, please download the **CP Clicker** app from your app store and point your device at images containing this symbol on the page numbers.

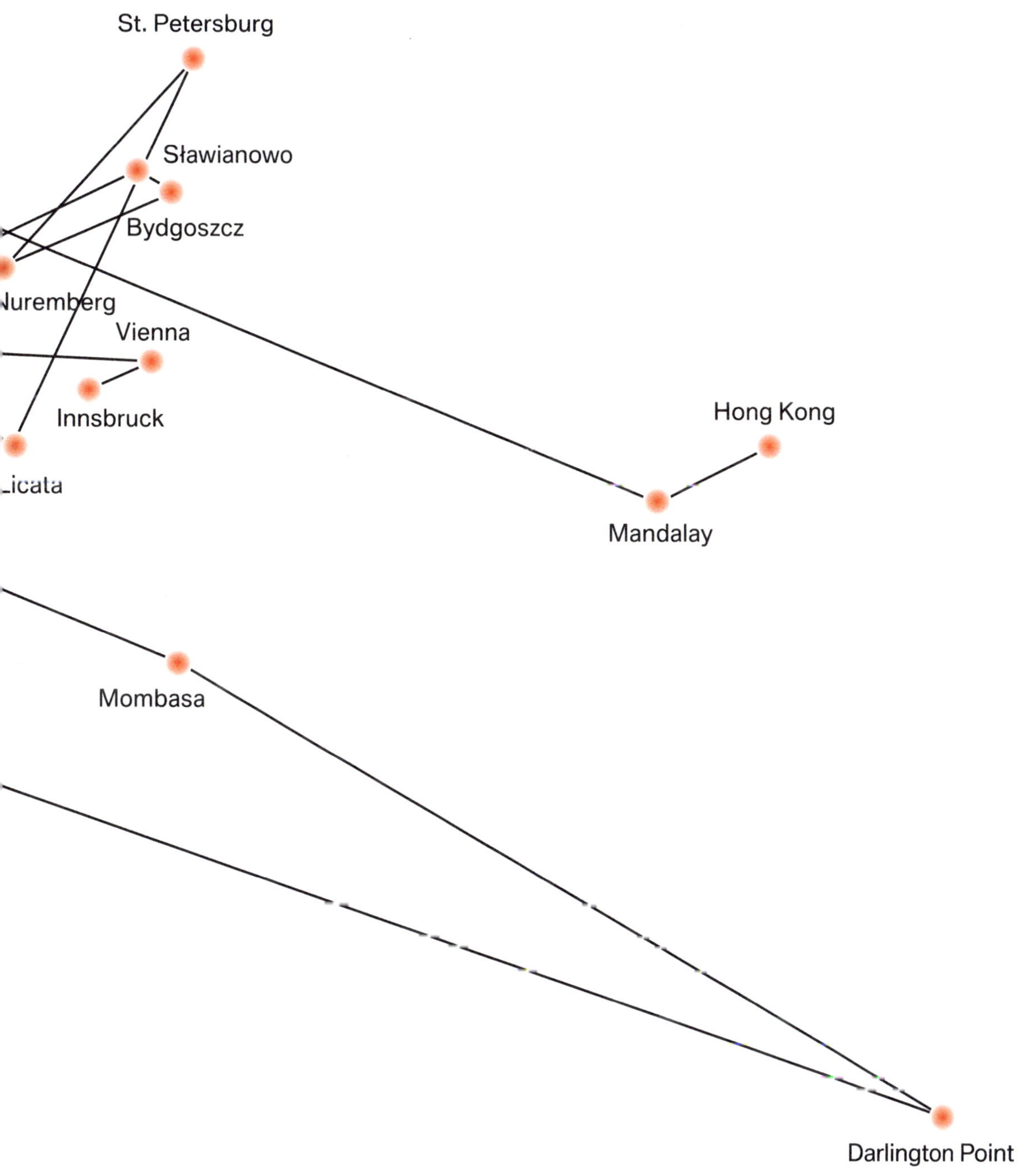

St. Petersburg
Sławianowo
Bydgoszcz
Nuremberg
Vienna
Hong Kong
Innsbruck
Licata
Mandalay
Mombasa
Darlington Point

On Bells and Cigarettes

I struggle to declare a transformation that might have taken place. In art writing we call this the artist's "decisive moment." With the benefit of hindsight, we may be tempted to flatten the passing of idle time into a critical juncture we call insight. But the only thing I can say for sure, at this point, is this: I developed an affinity for and embraced the disgusting habit of smoking during the bell-recording trip. I now see out of the corner of my eye an unopened packet, a bundle of death wishes on my writing desk, waiting to be ignited. I can certainly talk about *that*.

This is how it all started: *Bells don't ring for you*. There is a schedule, and you have to wait for them to ring. So to pass time I made sound sketches, and I smoked. But the "decisive moment" actually came earlier, at a dinner several months before I embarked upon the bell-recording trip where I proudly declared myself a social smoker. It's interesting to me that even the most unlikely smokers are compelled, even crave, to light a cigarette in social situations. Social smoking is aesthetically seductive: It is a beautiful ritual of communal death wishes, begetting an eloquent ballet of circular light, haze, and falling ash. Soldiers also smoke in groups: When cigarettes were distributed on the battlefield, it was a sign that an assault was imminent. Under fearful circumstances, smoking produces the conditions of prayer: We light a cigarette and hold it like a burning rosary.

There is a fundamental difference between fear and anxiety. Anxiety is an aura, like rising smoke under a floodlight, or an essential tremor of the hand that sets the world in motion, an inescapable condition of living that one nonetheless accepts and mitigates with vices like smoking. Fear is a sensory overload, like the camera's flashlight that is pointed toward an enemy, but at the same time it burns an afterimage on your retina. Instead of pacifying it, the cigarette exacerbates and externalizes fear with a pose: a small fire and a fist that is poised for a counter-strike.

The state takes pain to moderate our moral being by restricting the consumption of cigarettes when it has no control over extremists, lunatics with pistols, hateful politicians, and other administrators of fear. There was a time when growing up meant eliminating fears. But today, the ability to orchestrate and spread baseless fear takes on the appearance of emotional maturity, of wisdom, of foresight, even of moral strength. Fear has become the new solidarity.

And perhaps the greatest of all fears is the fear of oblivion.

Why do we tell stories?
Why do we leave messages?
Why do we send prayers?
Why do we give confessions?
Do stories rise like smoke?
Do messages fall like ashes?
Do prayers rise like smoke?
Do confessions fall like ashes?

To paraphrase Andrea Fraser, who in turn paraphrased Ross Bleckner, "remember me" is the urgent plea, the author's gentle whisper that is behind all creative acts: stories told, messages left behind, confessions made, prayers given, bells rung, and cigarettes lit. Whispering is the soul dripping with excess, a leakage that is between the certainty of speech and the inevitability of breath, an exhale that marks the beginning of the end.

Richard Klein, in *Cigarettes Are Sublime*, reasoned that smoking alone distinguishes humans from animals.

I hasten to add that music and art-making provide the same affirmation. Cigarettes and bells have this in common also: Their effects—the psychological resonance of the artifact—sustain a portal through which we may recognize, imagine, and sympathize with other consciousness. I am reminded of a scene from *For Whom the Bell Tolls*, in which Robert Jordan observed from afar the facial expression of an enemy as he enjoyed a charcoal-lit cigarette. The "friendly sameness of a compatriot's pleasure," the poeticism in the exhale of a hostile opponent, was too much to bear:

> The sentry sat leaning against the wall ... he took out a tobacco pouch and a packet of papers and rolled himself a cigarette. He tried to make a lighter work and finally put it in his pocket and went over to the brazier, leaned over, reached inside, brought up a piece of charcoal, juggled it in one hand while he blew on it, then lit the cigarette and tossed the lump of charcoal back into the brazier. Robert Jordan ... watched his face as he leaned against the box drawing on a cigarette ... I won't look at him again, he told himself.

> —Ernest Hemingway, *For Whom the Bell Tolls*

Art does nothing to "neutralize" the opponent. But in times like this, when the proliferation of fear turns every neighbor, shopkeeper, and collaborator into a suspect, may art always draw the enemy too close for comfort.

Myanmar

I spent the first three days of my journey in the city of Mandalay, in Myanmar, to record the Mingun Bell. This bell is significant not only because of its size, but because its construction involved thousands of slaves, who were also involved in the building of the never-finished Mingun Pagoda. That unpopular project contributed toward the dynasty's demise. I am interested in the close relationship between Buddhism and civic movements in this country, the most recent example, of course, being the monks' involvement and leadership in the Saffron Revolution of 2007. I recorded a bunch of temple bells at various locations, and I interviewed Buddhists who were involved in the protests. I also recorded the temple bell that sits on Mandalay Hill—the stage for one of the toughest battles of the Burma campaign during World War II. Aside from recording bells, I visited a third-generation bell craftsman's workshop. There I interviewed one of the members of the comedy trio Mustache Brothers, whose members were jailed for seven years for criticizing the military government in a performance at the home of Aung San Suu Kyi, in 1996. Par Par Lay was again arrested in 2007 during the Saffron Revolution.

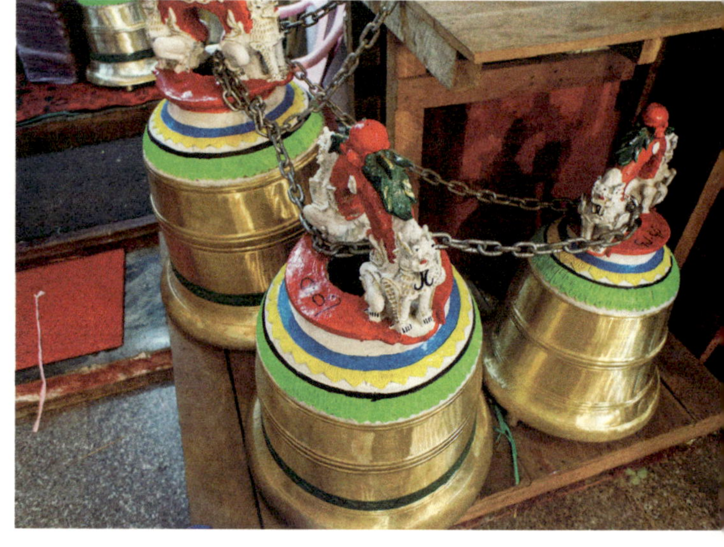

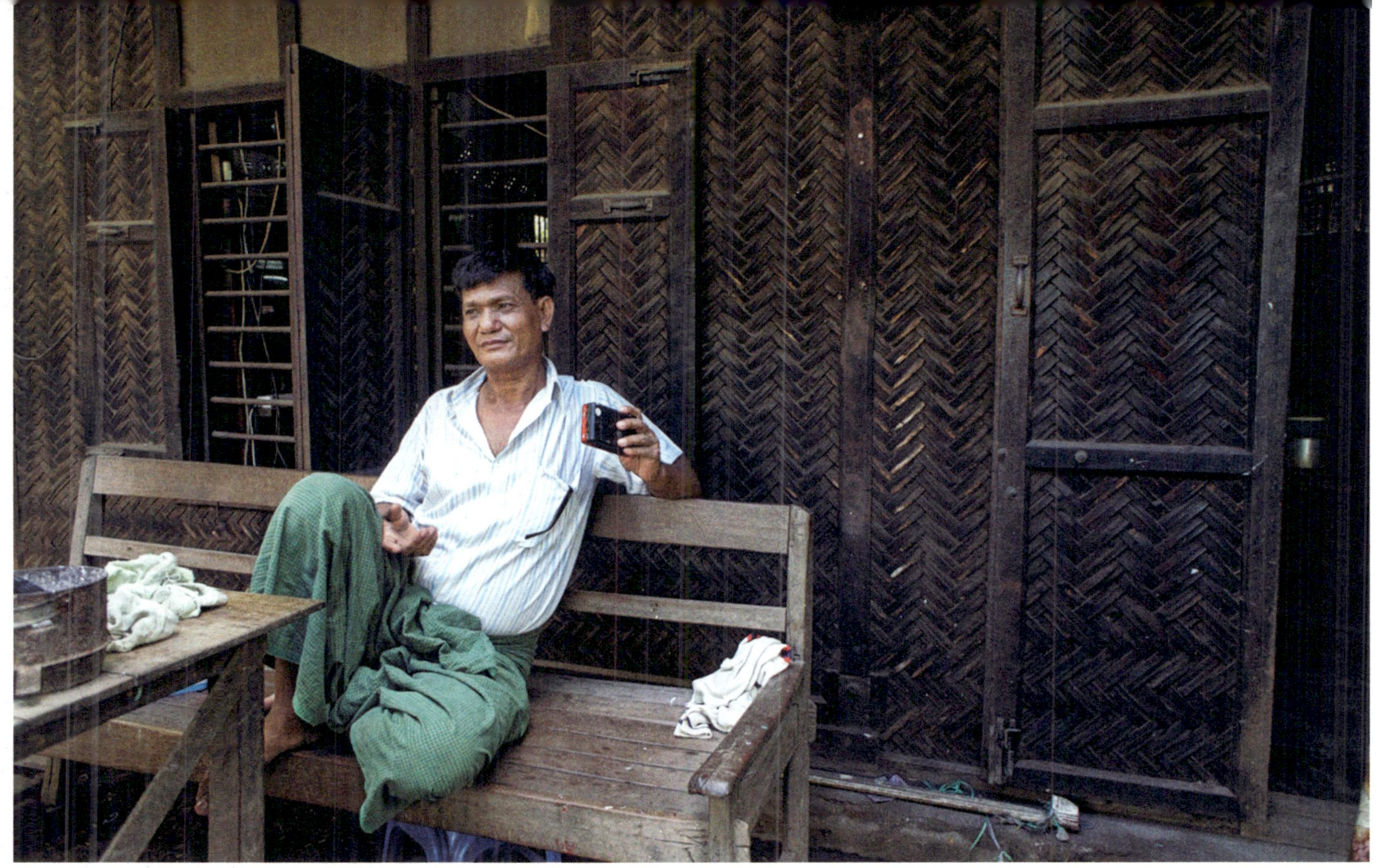

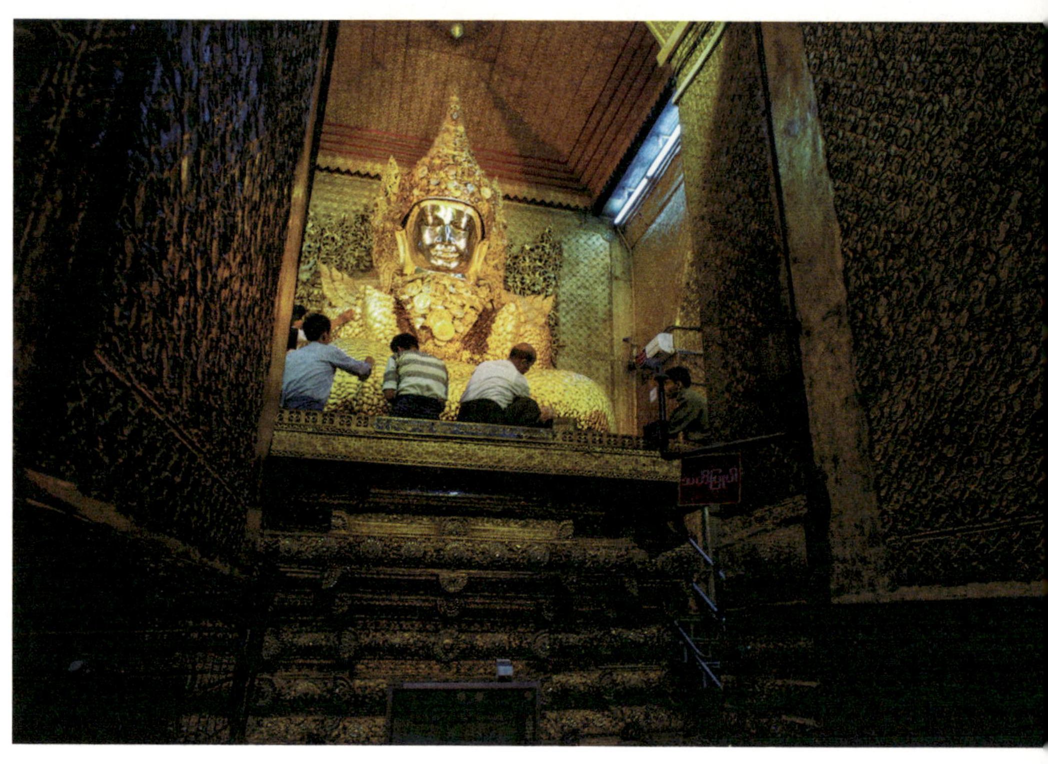

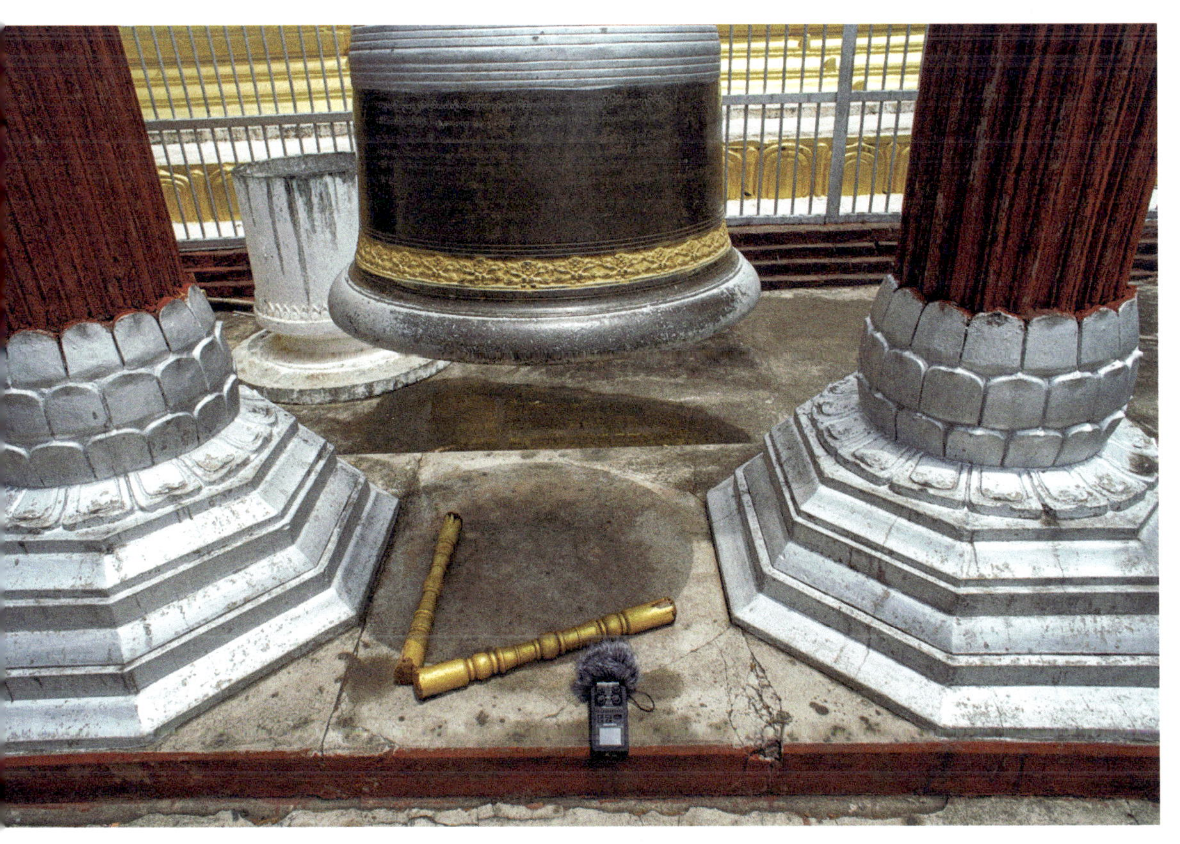

Myanmar

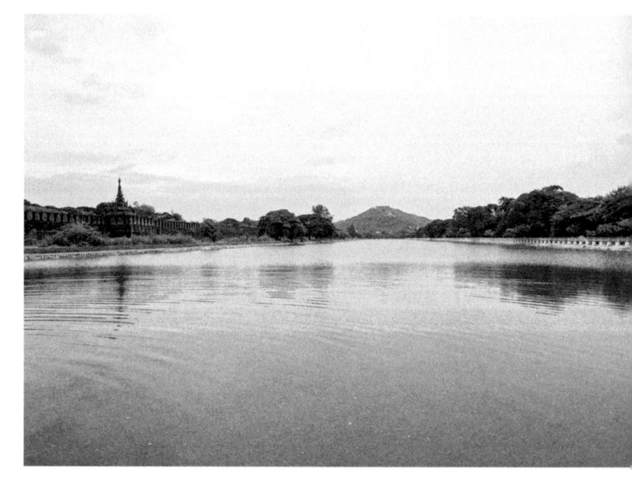

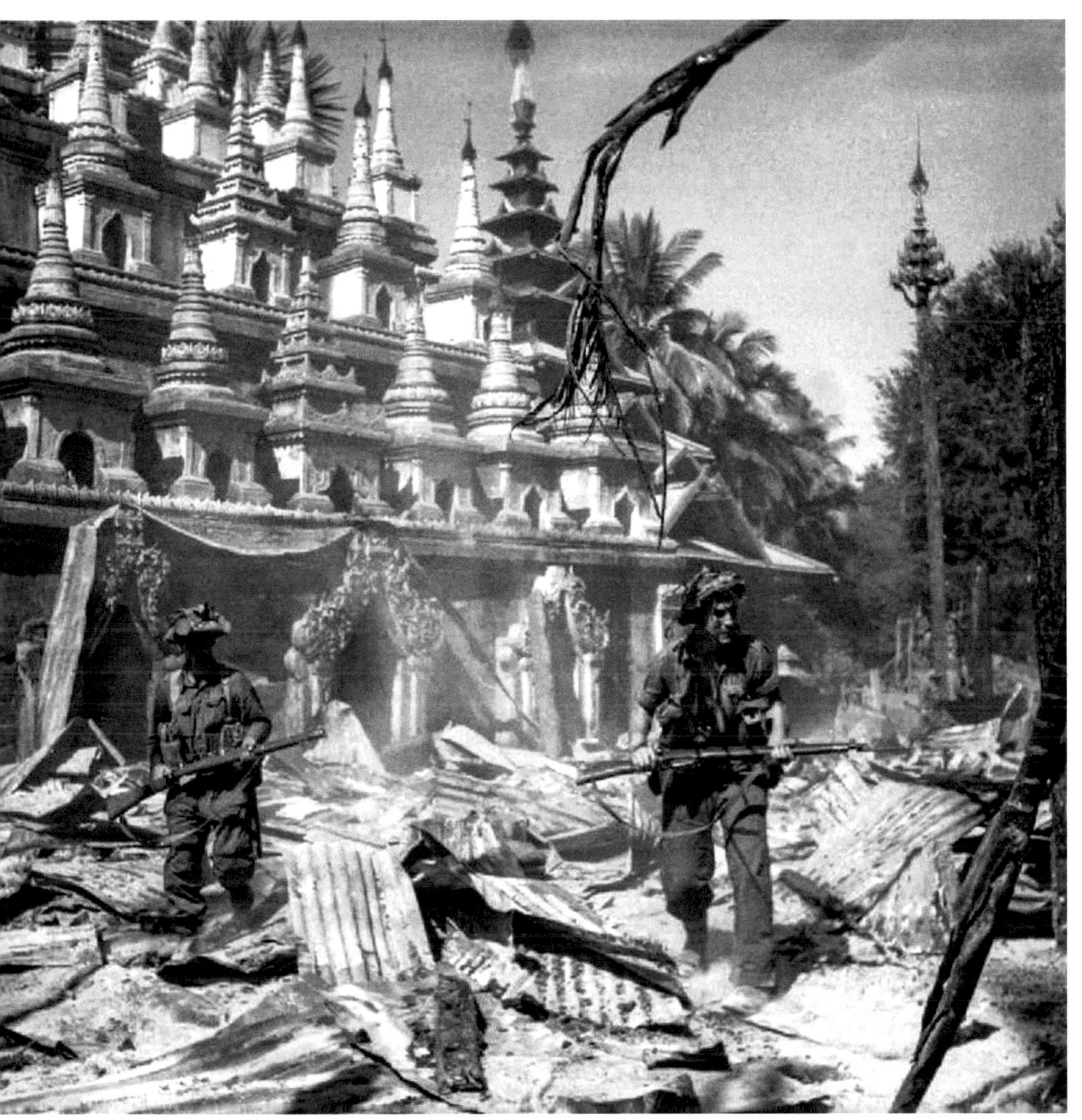

Myanmar

United
Kingdom

In London, I was introduced to the world of English-style change-ringing by two remarkable individuals.

Alan Regin is an experienced ringer and the steward of the Rolls of Honour at St Paul's Cathedral, which recorded the names of all known ringers who'd fallen in the two great wars. Alan showed me the two beautiful volumes that sit in a vitrine outside of the ringing chamber. The books were handcrafted by Timothy Noah and they are carefully maintained by Alan, with new names added frequently. Alan took me to other restricted-access areas, such as the room where the remains of the burnt-down portion of the cathedral are now stored. In the ringing chamber, we looked at the peal board that recorded the peal that was rung on the occasion of Queen Elizabeth's coronation. I sketched and recorded the sound of the Great Paul, the heaviest bell in the United Kingdom.

Alan is also the steeple-keeper of the Christ Church in Spitalfields. He got together a band of excellent ringers from all over U.K. for me to record, just hours after my arrival into the city. One of the men who rang that morning served in Northern Ireland during the turbulent years. He described to me how he would hear the bells ring on Sundays from his outpost, and wished that he were in the tower ringing instead of being on the ground.

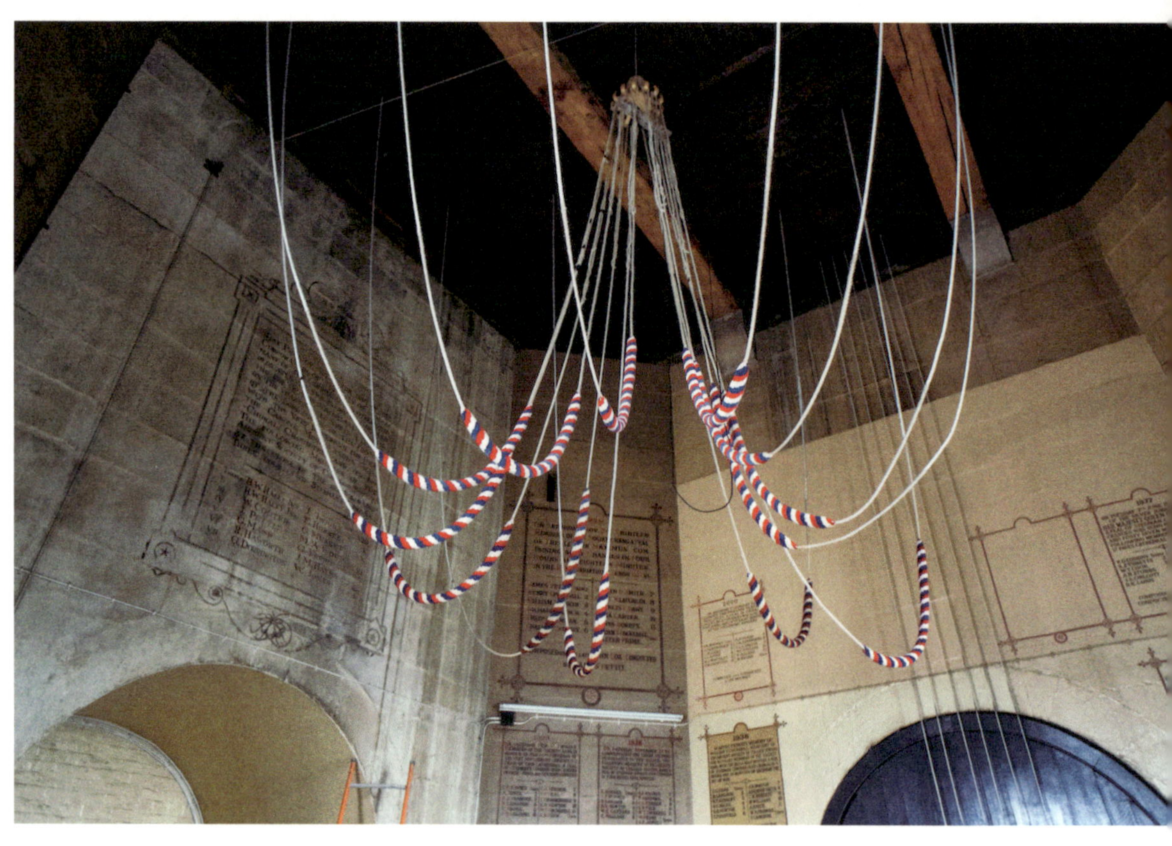

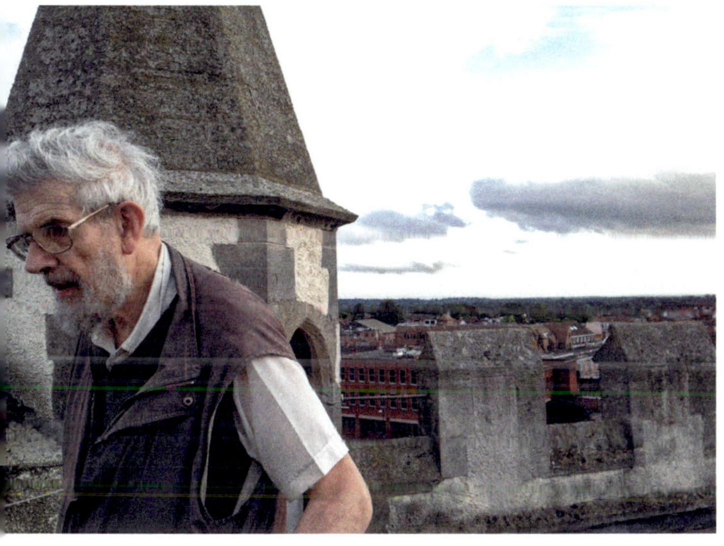

John Harrison was my initial entry point into the world of ringers. He is the steeple-keeper of the All Saints Church in Wokingham, where a ring of six bells was hung as early as 1704. I observed and recorded the Wokingham band's weekly practice session and witnessed how bell-ringing is taught to less experienced ringers.

The Great Paul, which adorns St. Paul's Cathedral in London, is the product of the John Taylor & Co. Bell Foundry. John Taylor invented a new way of bell-tuning that paid special attention to the harmonic complexity of the overtones produced. Before this innovation, bell-tuning was achieved by simply chipping away parts of the surfaces of a bell, which was crude and inaccurate. The foundry's history was intertwined with the history of warfare. Two of the family's descendants perished on the battlefields of the Great War. A great number of memorial carillons across the United Kingdom and the United States were cast by John Taylor & Co. One such example is the War Memorial Carillons at Queens Park in Loughborough, which are sounded on Thursday and Sunday afternoons in the summer months.

The foundry keeps an excellent archive, which has recorded the inscriptions on all of the bells produced by the firm since 1930. In many cases, the inscriptions offer details about the donors who provided patronage for the casting of the bells. From the second half of the 1940s right through to the 1950s, a great many bells bore inscriptions that paid tribute to the fallen in the war.

My final destination in the United Kingdom before departing for Germany was Canterbury Cathedral, in Kent. The cathedral is home to the ship's bell that served the HMS *Canterbury*, a C-class light cruiser of the Royal Navy that participated in one of the toughest naval battles of the First World War. Every weekday at 11 a.m., the ship's bell is rung and a page on the book of remembrance is turned.

I started reading Anne Frank's diary again. Something that I'd completely missed in my previous reading: the bells in the Westertoren, which the annex residents would have heard every hour on the hour, until they went silent sometime in 1943, when many bells were removed and melted down. In isolation, the bells punctuated Anne's time in confinement and made the experience a little more bearable.

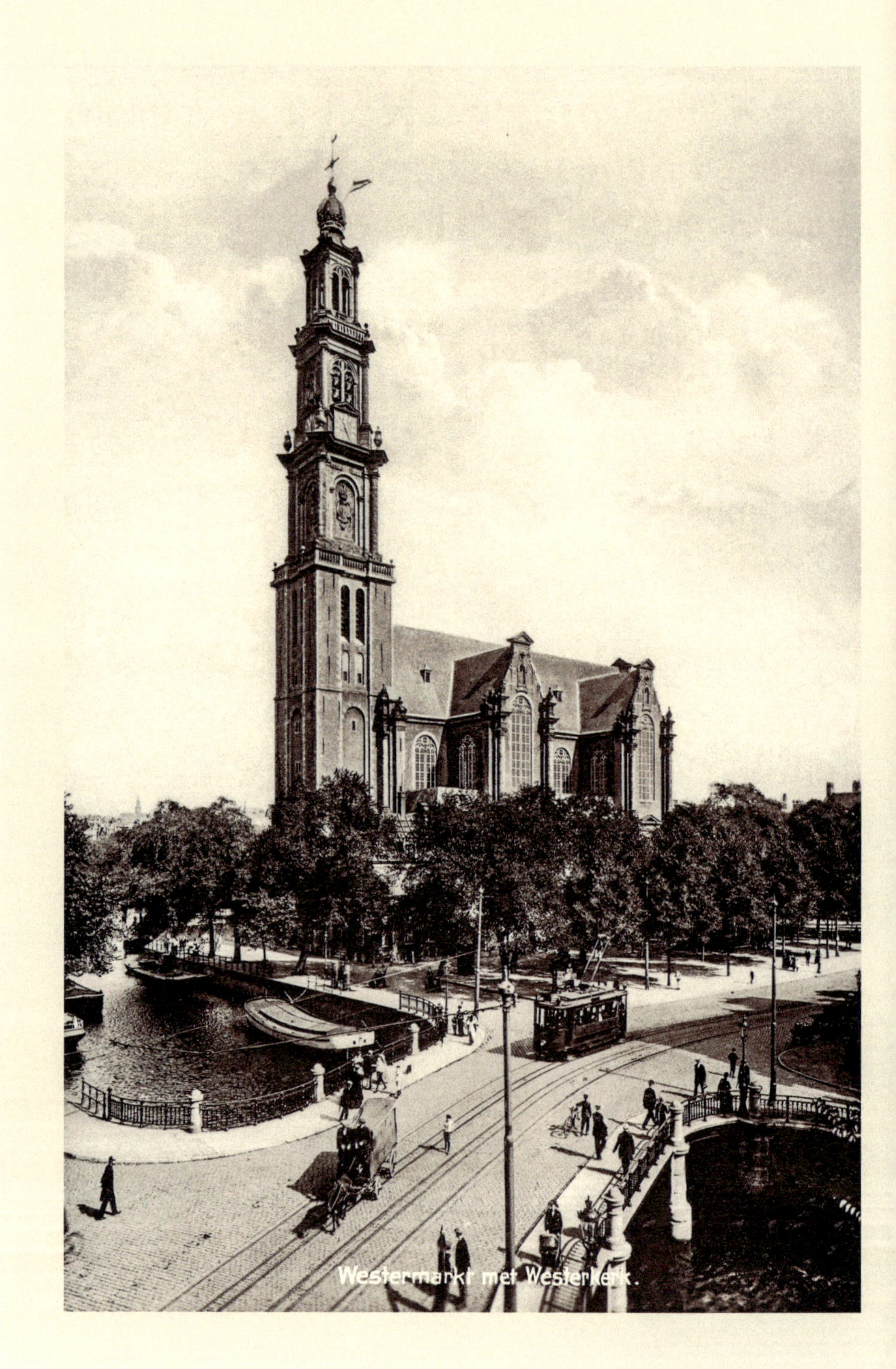

Westermarkt met Westerkerk.

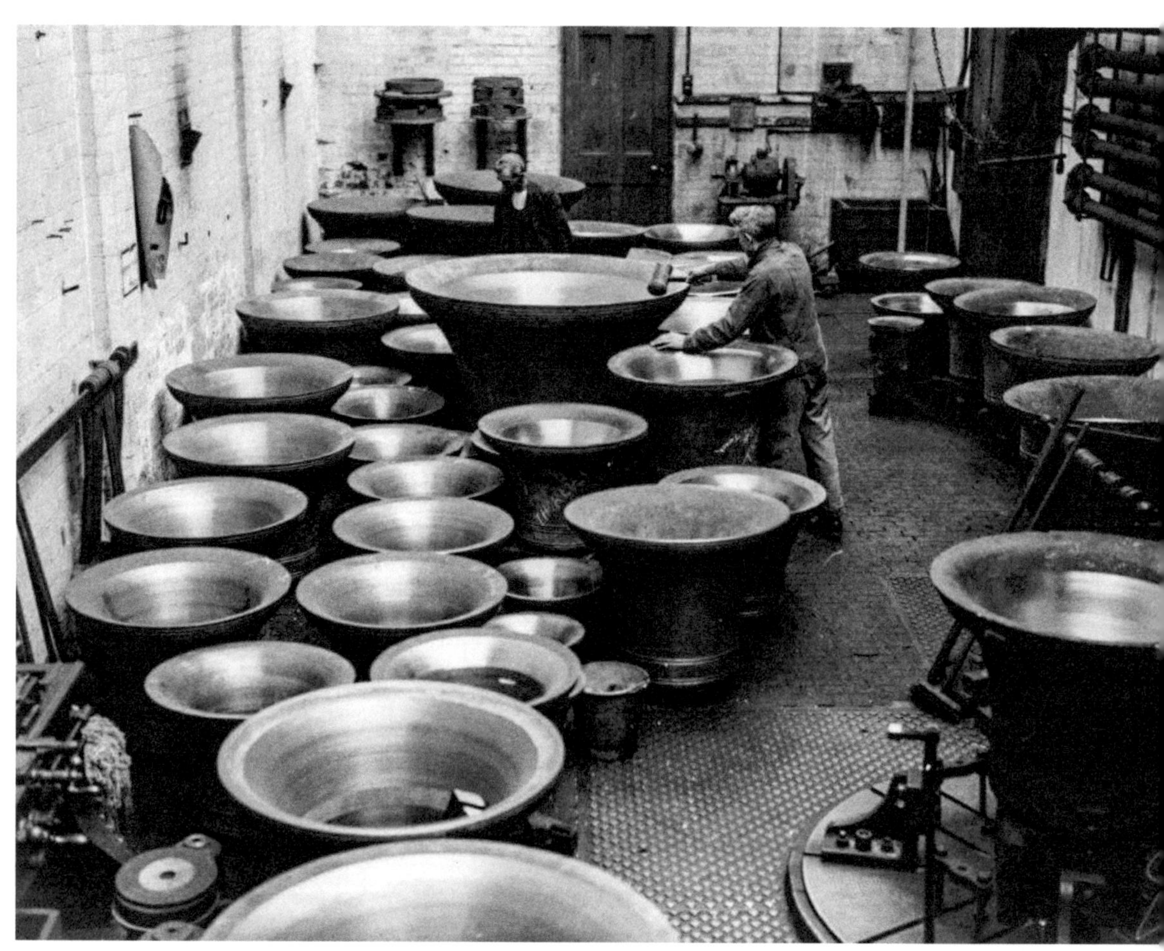

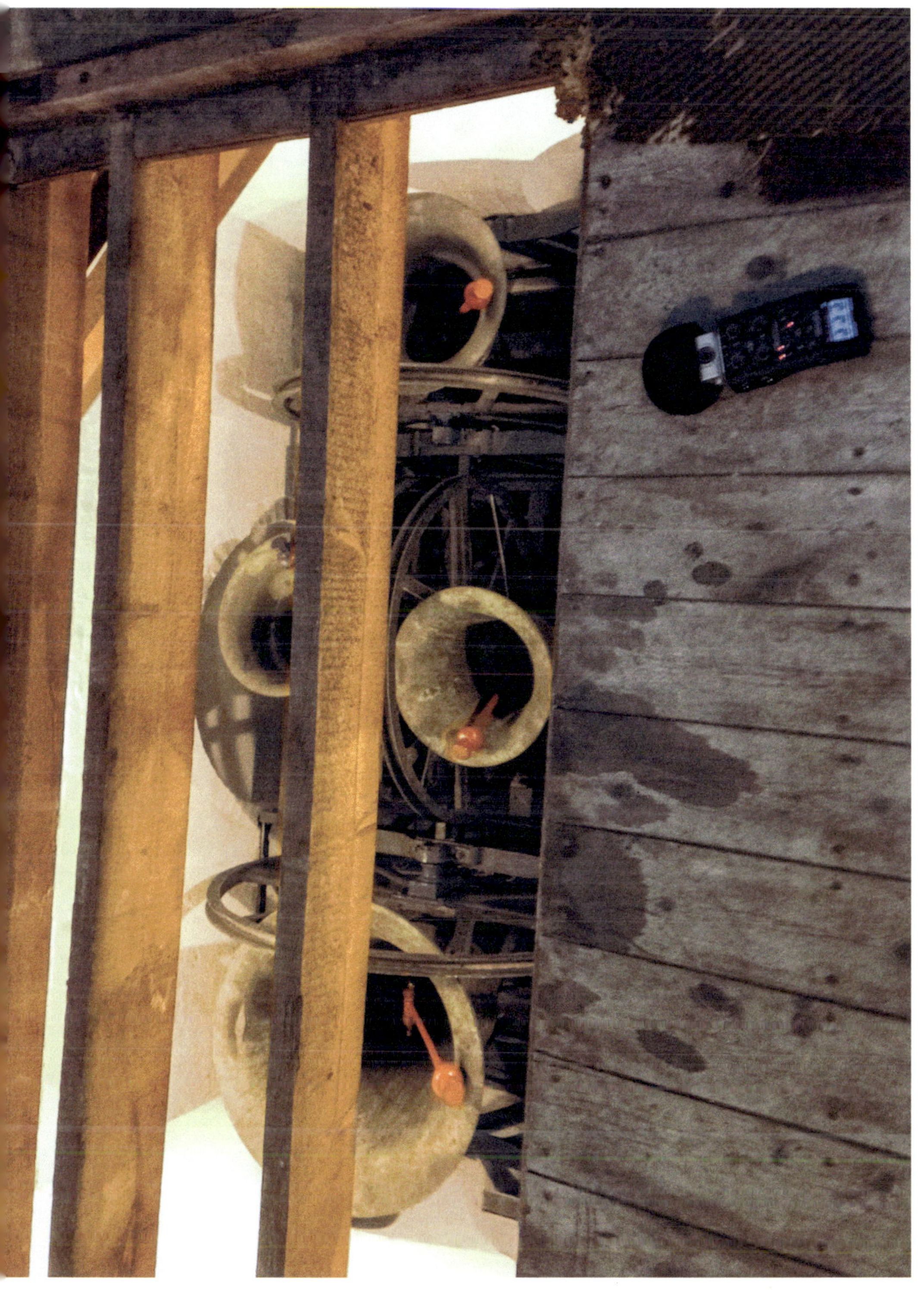

United Kingdom

Germany
Poland

I traveled from Nuremberg to Bydgoszcz to track down a bell that was confiscated by the Nazis and survived the war. Shortly after the Second World War broke out, the Nazis calculated the amount of resources that would be required to realize their objectives and figured that metal would soon be in short supply. A comprehensive plan was drawn up to acquire additional metal by confiscating church bells from all over Germany and the annexed territories. Bells were forcefully removed, transported, and temporarily stored in a shipyard (later nicknamed "the bell cemetery") near the city of Hamburg. There the bells awaited their fate. In an attempt to preserve the more significant bells, well-meaning local authorities submitted every single one of them to a systematic process of examination and categorization. They produced an index card for each bell, a sort of preemptive "death certificate" that noted the bell's origin, date of production, weight, pitch, and ornamental features, such as inscriptions. Pencil presses and plaster molds of bell inscriptions were made. Based on these recorded characteristics, each bell was then given a rating of A, B, C, or D, with D being the least significant and thus ready to be immediately melted down for metal. The index cards eventually ended up in the archives of Nuremberg's Germanisches Nationalmuseum.

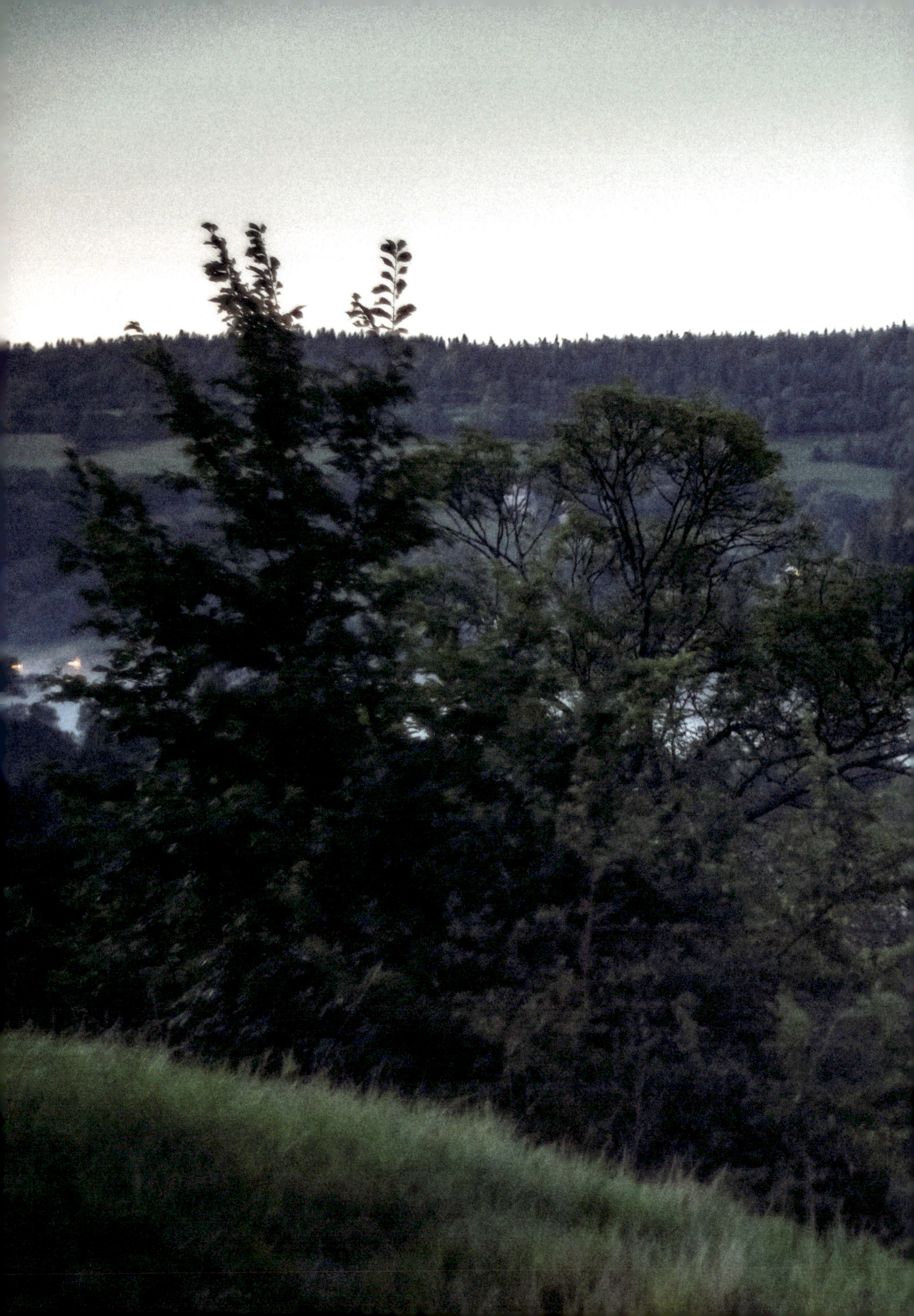

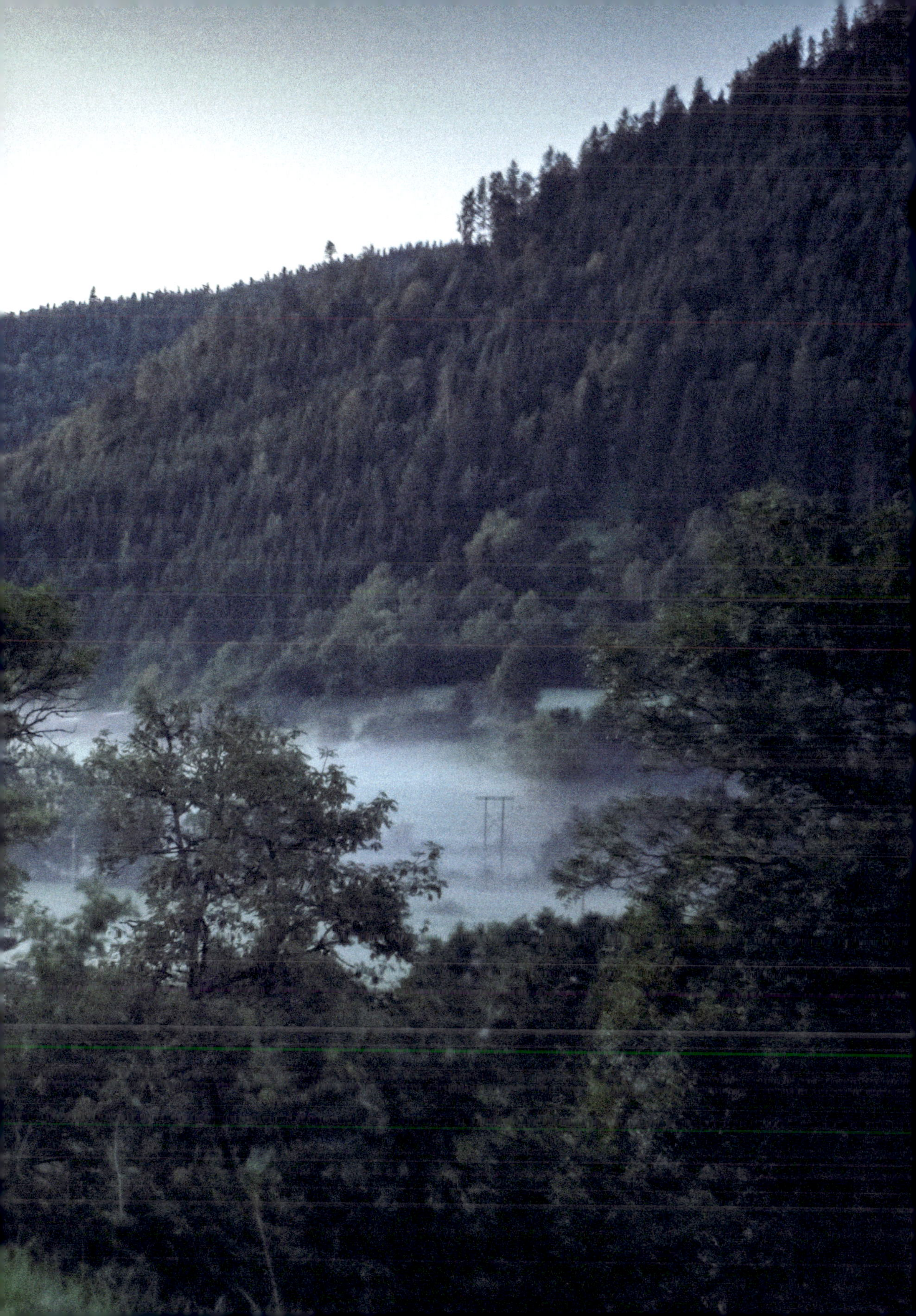

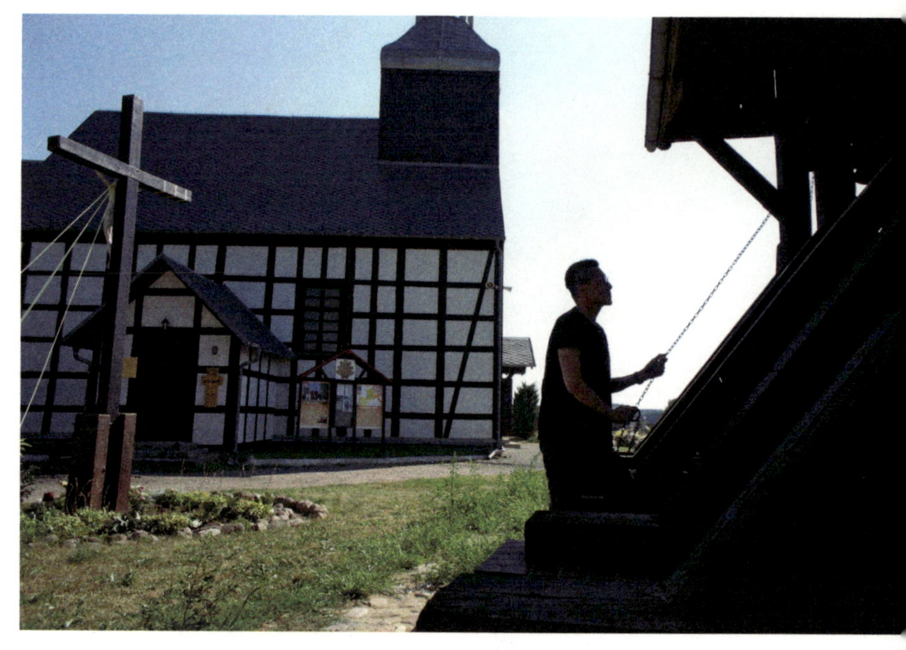

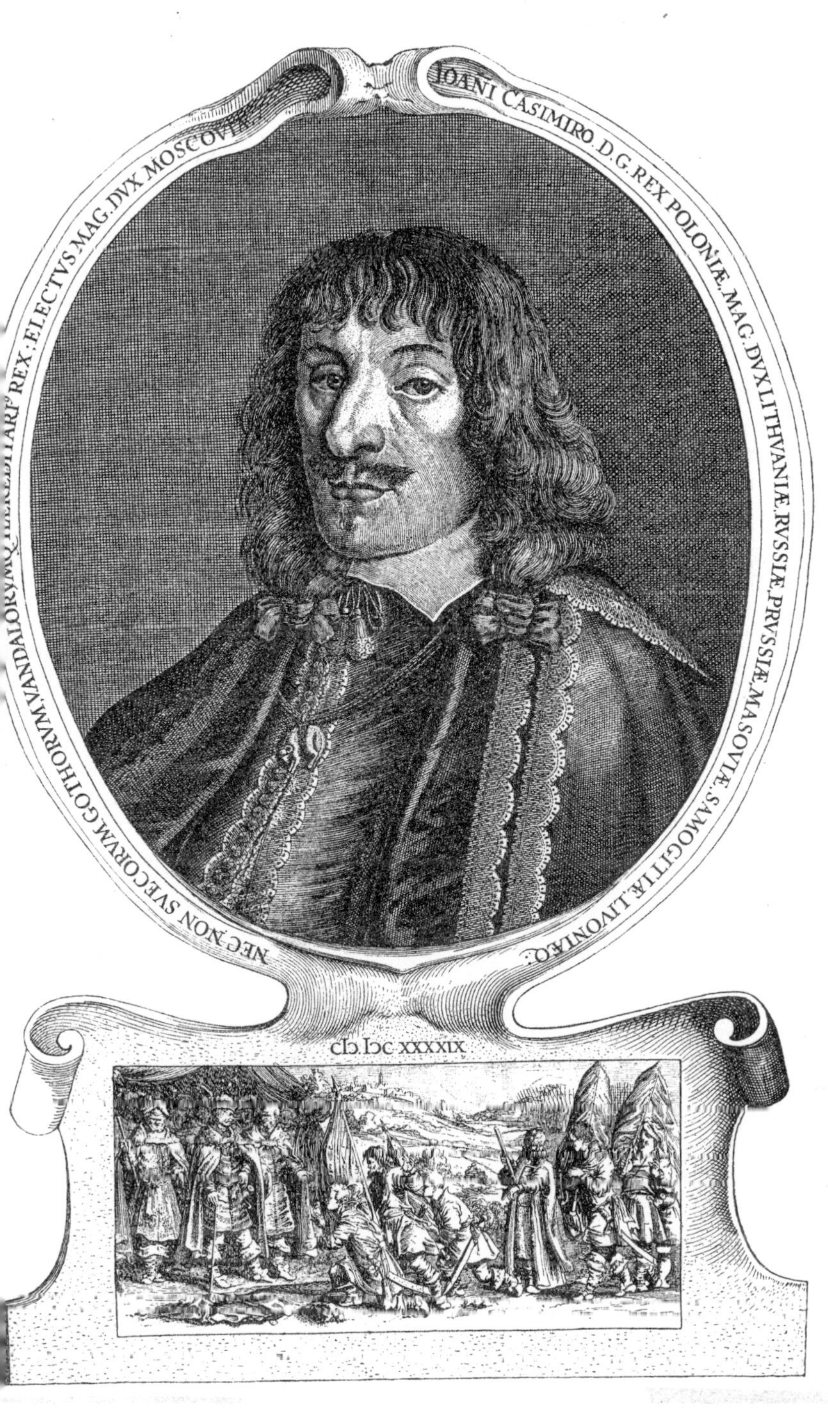

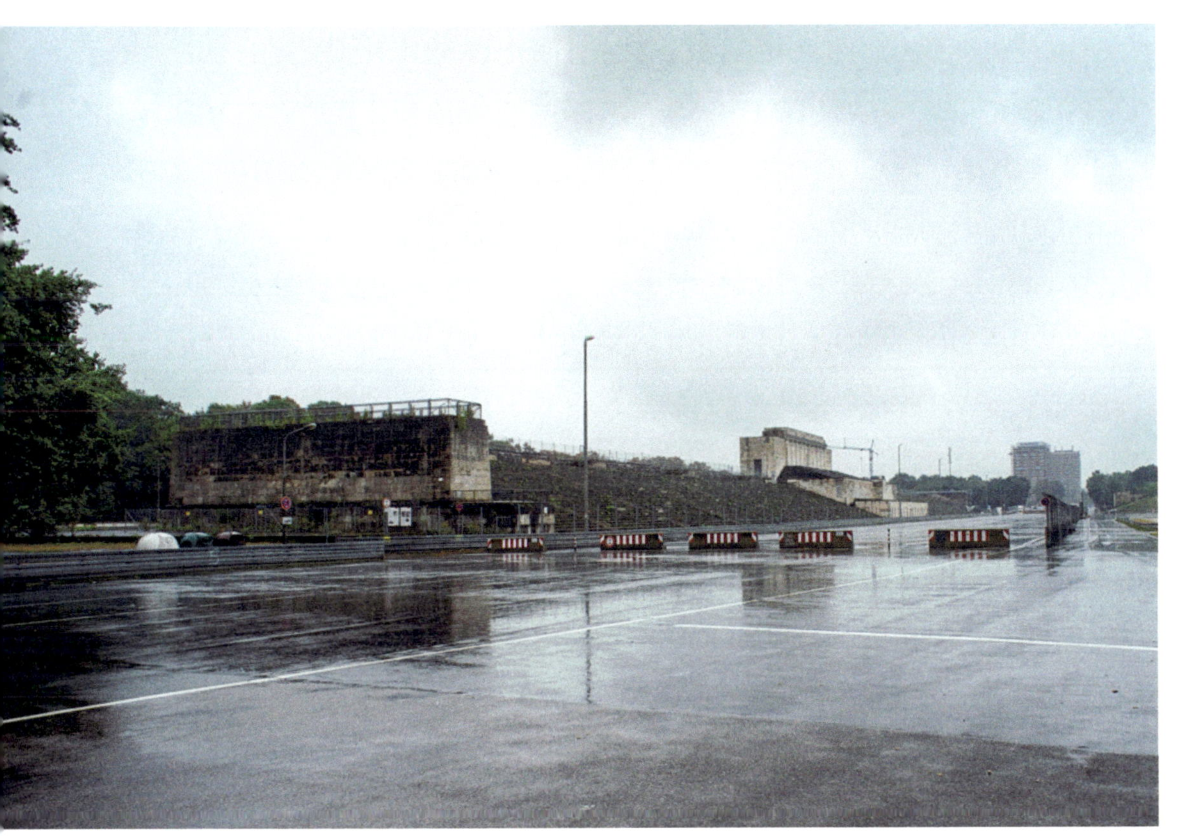

A great number of bells classified as C or above survived the war. The German bells were, in most cases, returned to their respective places of origin. Bells from the annexed territories were not so lucky. A court ruling dictated that the thefts of bells from Poland and other places were "merely acts of war." By virtue of this ruling, all confiscated bells essentially became German national property. Few people cared at that point. Europe was in ruins, and there were more pressing issues to worry about. Bells from the annexed territories were sent somewhat indiscriminately to German churches that cared to ask for them. A 2004 article in *Die Zeit* covered the story of a dispute between a Polish parish and a German church over the ownership of one such confiscated bell. After much digging and a few phone calls, and with the help of a German friend, Matthias, and his Polish-speaking friend, Joanna, we discovered that the bell had been returned to its rightful owner in 2005, to the tiny village of Sławianowo, which sits on the outskirts of Bydgoszcz, in Poland.

On this trip, I first visited the bell archive at the Germanisches Nationalmuseum. The index cards were beautifully made. To my surprise, the museum had kept many bell fragments. Apparently, the bell cemetery was bombed by the Allies, and some of the important bells were destroyed.

Dr. Matthias Nuding, the archive's director, told me that I was the first person to look at these fragments since their transfer to the museum. I carefully photographed, measured, and recorded the ring of each fragment. In Nuremberg, I also recorded the clock bell of the Frauenkirche from the market, where Hitler was seen addressing his troops in Leni Riefenstahl's *Triumph of the Will*. I made several field recordings at the Zeppelinfeld Nazi rally grounds.

I then went to Poland to see the stolen bell in the Church of St. James the Apostle, in Sławianowo. The head priest was kind enough to let me ring the bell. The next day, the guide took me to the Bydgoszcz district of Fordon, near the infamous "Valley of Death." We visited an abandoned synagogue there, where I made some recordings and interviewed a local resident who is fundraising to revive the synagogue. He told me a remarkable story: At one time, a sizable Jewish population resided in the district. The Swedish king John II Casimir Vara, ruling Poland at that time, established Fordon as a "model community," where Jews, Catholics, and Protestants would live harmoniously alongside each other. This aspiration is still evident in the city's plan. The majority of the Jews, however, fled before the war; only twenty-eight remained, and they worked together to maintain the synagogue until all were sent to the concentration camps. Out of these twenty-eight Jews, only a single one survived the war. This lone survivor came back to the district in the 1950s, in the hope of rejoining her community, only to discover that none of her friends and neighbors had survived—an entire community wiped out. Many believe that she then left the country and never returned. Others, however, believe that she adopted a new, non-Jewish identity and continues to live in the district to this day.

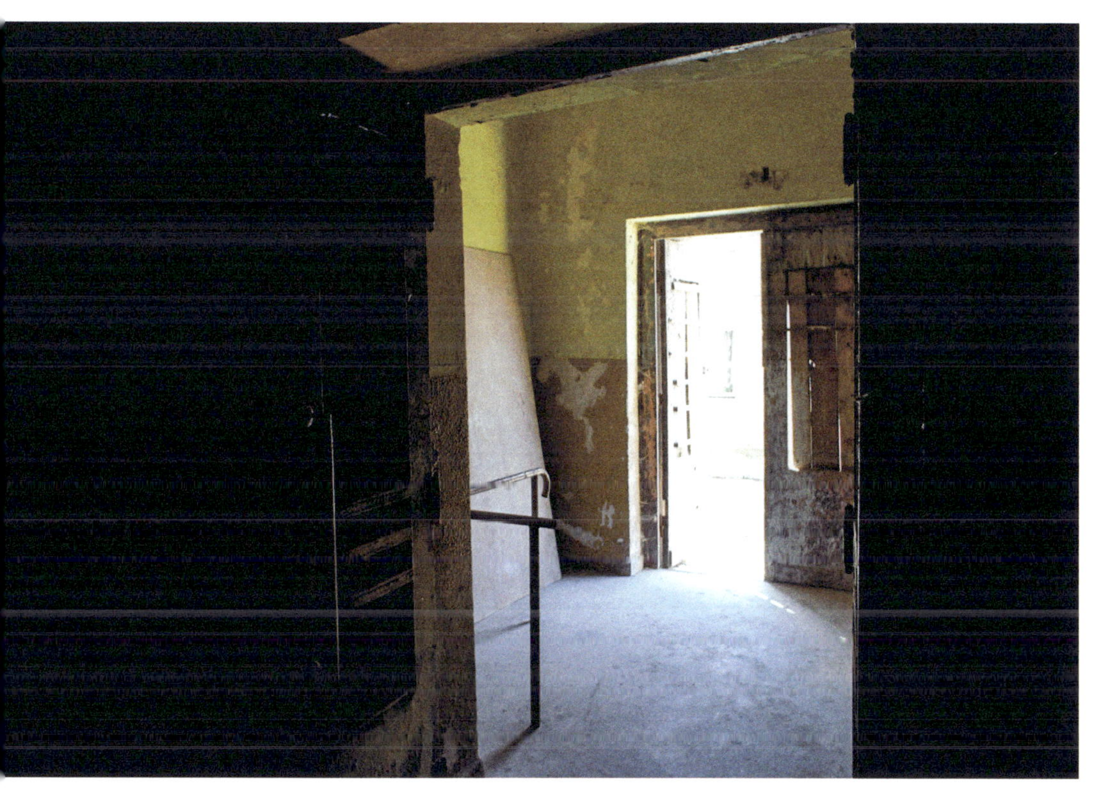

France

I came to France to enter into the sound world of the
post-Enlightenment French countryside, as depicted
in Alain Corbin's *Les cloches de la terre*—which, in my
opinion, is one of the most important publications on
nineteenth-century European micro-history, and a case
of historicizing through the auditory. Corbin's book
serves as a philosophical point of departure for the
journey that I am undertaking.

Another work of literature that underpinned this part of
the journey is Iris Murdoch's *The Bell*, which I picked up
in London. I turned the last page in Cantal. *The Bell* is
about people's struggles to define goodness in a world
in which our spiritual and moral beings—in the absence
of God—depended on religious structures that the society as a whole had long outgrown. The novel's narrative
unfolds through the consciousness of several characters.
English poet A. S. Byatt once said that one of Murdoch's
abiding lessons was "the difficulty and necessity of imag-
ining other people, with centres of consciousness as real
as our own, and different." Yes, obviously, and more ur-
gently so than ever before—but how does one actually
go about attempting this?

In Rouen I tried to explain to Pete and Stephen—who had joined me to document the journey—the reason behind my choice of color for a certain sound in my sound drawings. I soon realized that this was an impossible exercise: How can I make you hear C major as a light, transparent yellow? (Pete's C major, he told me, is blue.) What we could agree on was the idea of hearing in colors—that there is a consistency to the structure of this peculiar experience that is specific to each individual. Here, effective communication seems improbable, but I have always thought that communication is overrated.

What we need is an awareness of one another's consciousness and empathy for the peculiar predicaments of others. And there are perhaps few better ways to get into another person's head than through a sound with a long decay. With me, listen to this: A bell is struck; a wave of metallic articulations slowly pierces through space. A ringing resonance lingers long after the abrupt percussive event, like the persistent afterimage of a camera's flash. The surplus, the residual, of this sensory overload that burns our sonic retina sustains in us a portal to one another's minds. An infinitely extended reverberation binds us in a consensual hallucination, which dissolves only when we allow our imaginations to become disengaged.

Back to nineteenth-century France: Corbin described a world in which the sound of these large sonorous objects defined territories, punctuated secular and religious time, marked life events, and called citizens to arms. Bells were among the rare objects at rural folks' disposal that they believed they could deploy against the inexorable forces of nature, including plagues and storms.

Corbin made frequent references to the department of Cantal, in south-central France, where people believed in the magical power of bells to cast off thunderstorms. So deeply rooted was this belief that the practice of ringing in a thunderstorm continued for well over a century after laws that prohibited it had already been put in place. Corbin described the economy of bells in these small communities. Evidently, individuals were charged significant sums of money for ringing a bell at important life events, such as a wedding or funeral. In some villages, the richer inhabitants sponsored the casting of "public bells" that tolled for all without reward. On such occasions the whole community rallied. Rich and poor came together to contribute what they could. Family jewels and cheap household metallic objects alike were thrown into the furnace. A public bell was the crystallization of a community's collective aspiration.

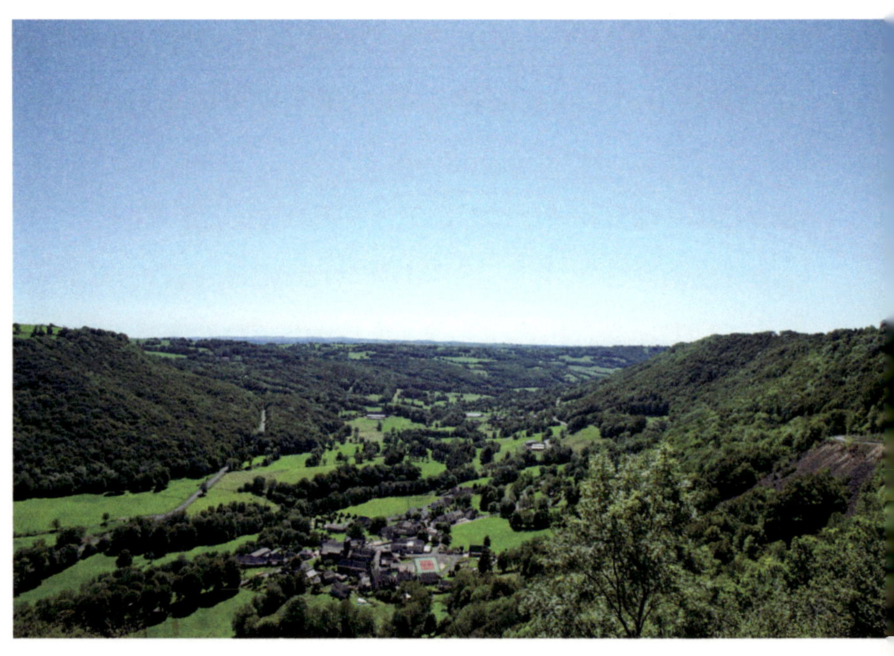

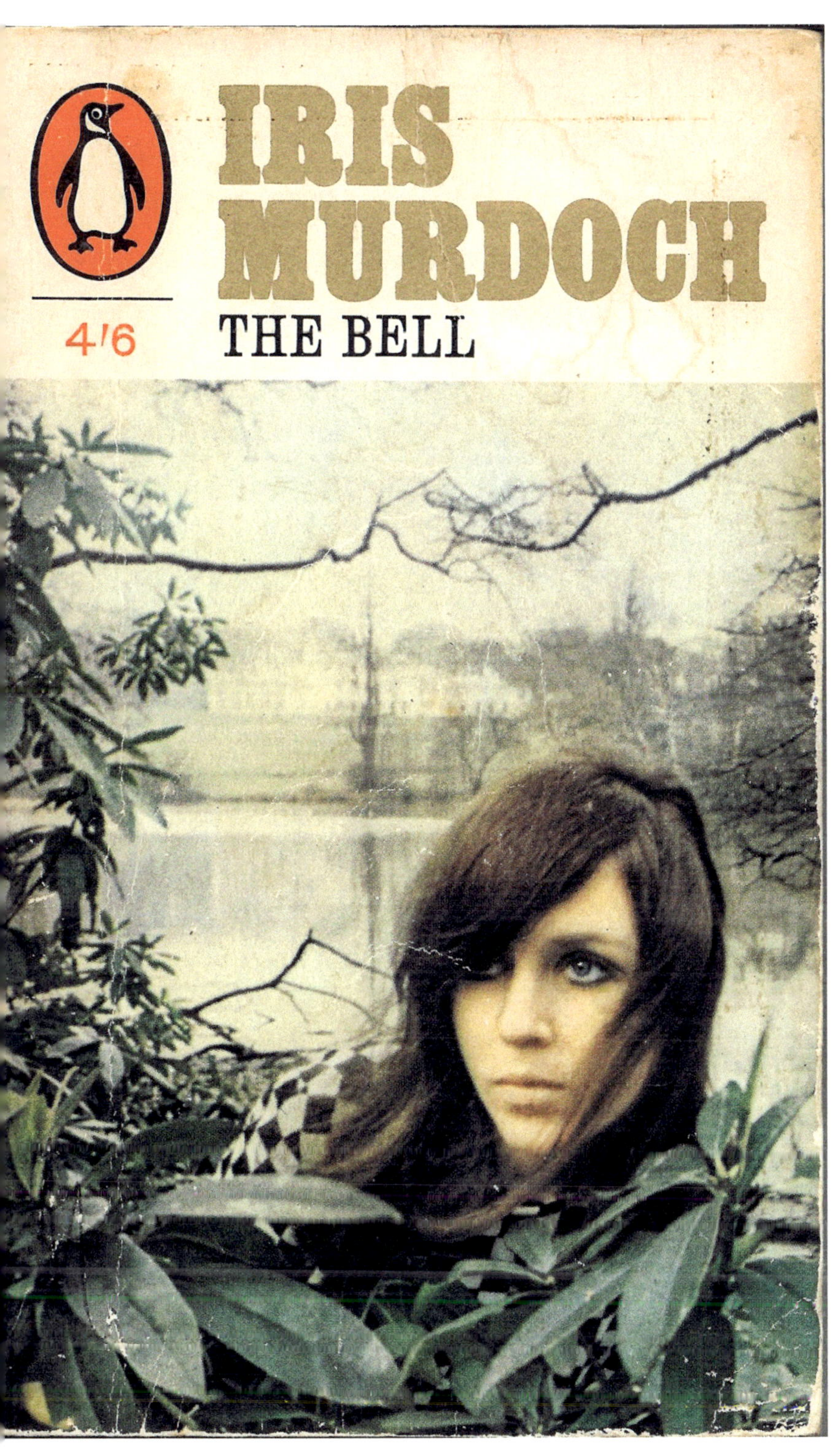

France

53

On August 24, we left Rouen for Cantal, where the party was joined by art historian and manager Thomas Girst. I had wished to visit three bells: a public bell at l'Église Saint-Hilaire de Brezons; a "magic bell" *(la cloche magique)* that was believed to possess special powers against thunder, at Vigouroux; and a public bell at l'Église de Saint-Martin sous Vigouroux that bears the inscription, "I shall ring for the rich as well as the poor." After some initial uncertainties, and with the help of our local guide, Beatrice, we managed to locate and record all three of the bells.

We also visited the village of Labrousse, where in 1831 a fight broke out between villagers who held contrasting views about the tolling of the village bell. One side believed that the bell's sound encouraged thunderstorms, while the other believed the exact opposite. I had read about this in an article in passing. There was mention of bloodshed in the church, but I did not harbor any hope that the villagers would have any awareness of this. Upon our arrival in Labrousse, we encountered, as if by divine intervention, local historians Lucie and Claude Gard, who had, as it turned out, written about the *bataille* in their book, *Monographie de Labrousse*. Among the other remarkable individuals we encountered were local archaeologist Annie Rassinot and her husband, who generously shared knowledge of bells in Cantal and showered us with French hospitality; the many mayors who brought us into the beautiful churches and bell towers; and the innkeeper at Vigouroux, who sang for us an Occitan folk song about a bell that had fallen into a lake—coincidentally the premise of Murdoch's book.

In times of extreme and stormy weather, in churches along the coast and deep in the mountains, bells tolled for the lost traveler like sonic beacons of bright light. Scientist Charles Babbage once speculated that sounds never disappear entirely after an articulation, but are instead archived in the air, as imprints on the atmosphere's particles, as "testimonies of man's changeful will."

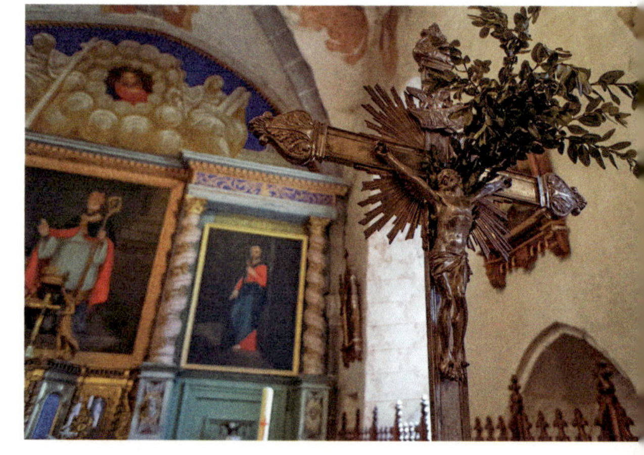

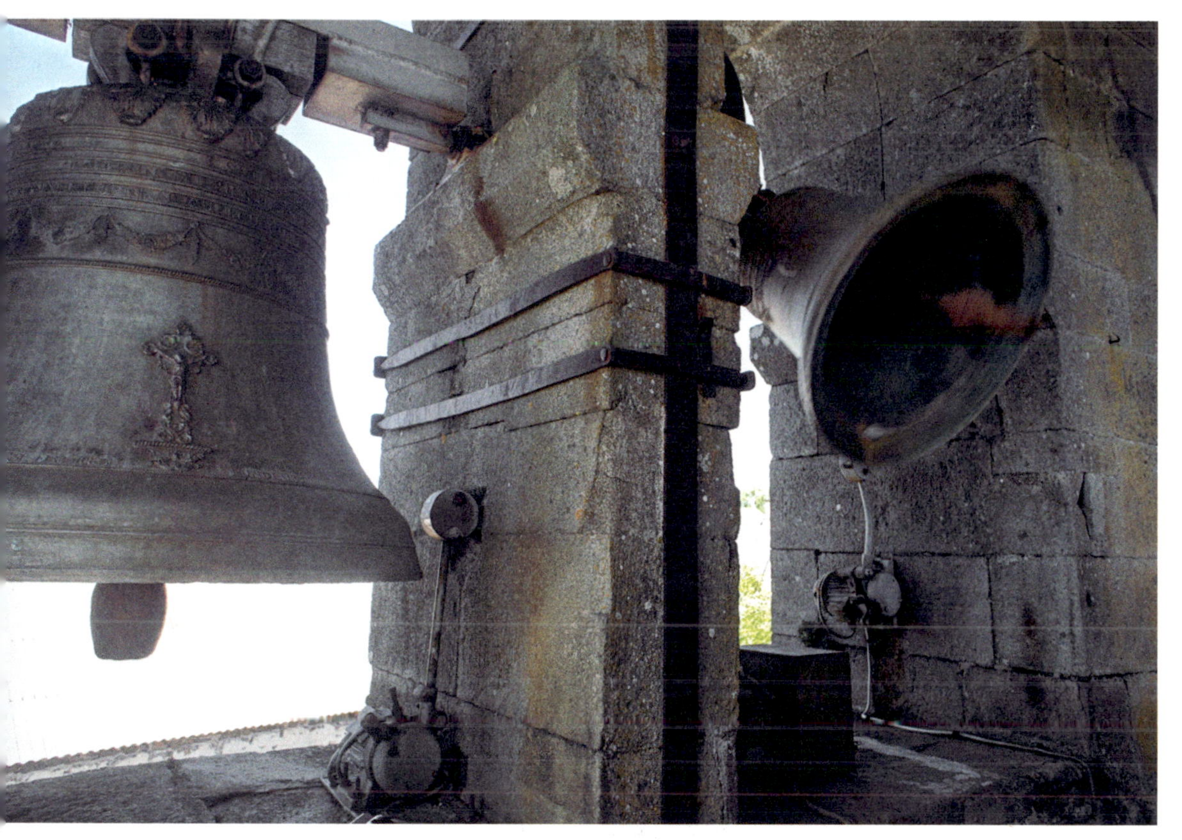

France

Italy

My search for bells brought me to the fishing town of
Licata, in southern Sicily. We were observing one of the
hottest Italian summers on record. The air here had a smell
of burnt diesel and rotten fish. The serene beaches that
dot the coastline of Licata were among the key military objectives of Operation Husky, in World War II.

There are different ways of looking at a landscape. One
could focus on its beauty. One could also see the terrors
of the forces of nature. In 1943, writer and journalist John
Hersey accompanied the Allied forces on their Sicilian
landing as a war correspondent. Returning to America
a transformed man, Hersey wrote his first novel, *A Bell
for Adano*, which won him a Pulitzer Prize. A cinematic
adaptation starring John Hodiak and Gene Tierney soon
followed. While Hemingway's "paper wars" (his words)
are full of grisly and realistic details, Hersey's painted ro-
mantic and idealized pictures of good people in the worst
of times. Adano—a fictional Italian coastal city that was
modeled after Licata—has lost its city-hall bell to the
Fascists. When the Allied forces roll in, more than food,
shelter, or anything else, the people of Adano demand
a new bell. Without their bell, they do not know when to
bake, to drive, or to work the field.

Hersey's fictional city bell was based on an actual seven-hundred-year-old bell that once adorned the Palazzo di Città in Licata, which was melted down by Mussolini for metal and restored after the war. I spent most of my time making recordings and sound sketches of the city bell. I also recorded the bells at the Cathedral of Saint Angelo —the town's patron saint. In Hersey's novel, it is through an appearance at the Sant'Angelo that Major Joppolo, the main protagonist of the story, gains the trust of the people of Adano. Among the other locations where I made recordings were Palazzo San Girolamo, the Poliscia Beach, a public square near Cappella de Cristo Nero, and the Castle of Sant'Angelo.

Both the novel and its Hollywood adaptation would come across as historically presumptuous to the contemporary viewer. They were products of a time when the people of America needed reassurance. Today, warfare is widely broadcast via various media outlets, around the clock in live streams of seductive and terrifying sounds and images. Those of us living in large cities do not directly experience the visceral realities of armed conflict. I am reminded to tread lightly between the romanticization of warfare and the sort of knee-jerk judgements that art has no place in making. The truth is probably somewhere in the contradiction. At Sant'Angelo, to my initial horror, the 5 p.m. "bell" was a severely distorted recording emitted from low-quality speakers. But after a while I found it to be a rather musical discord.

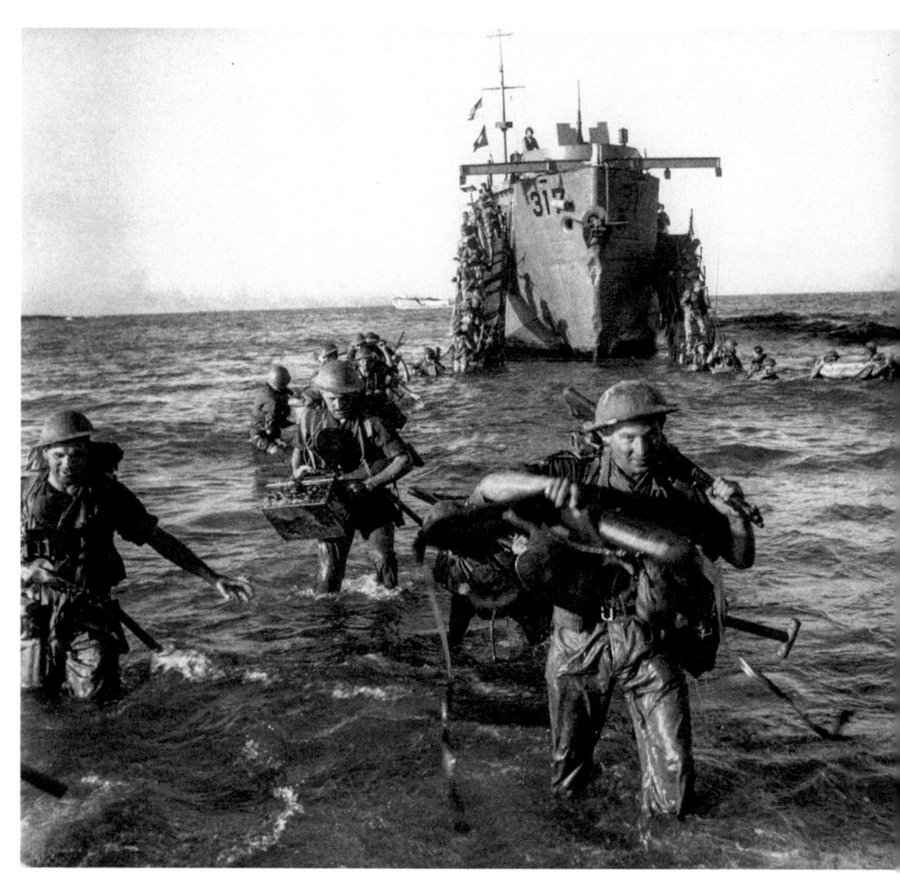

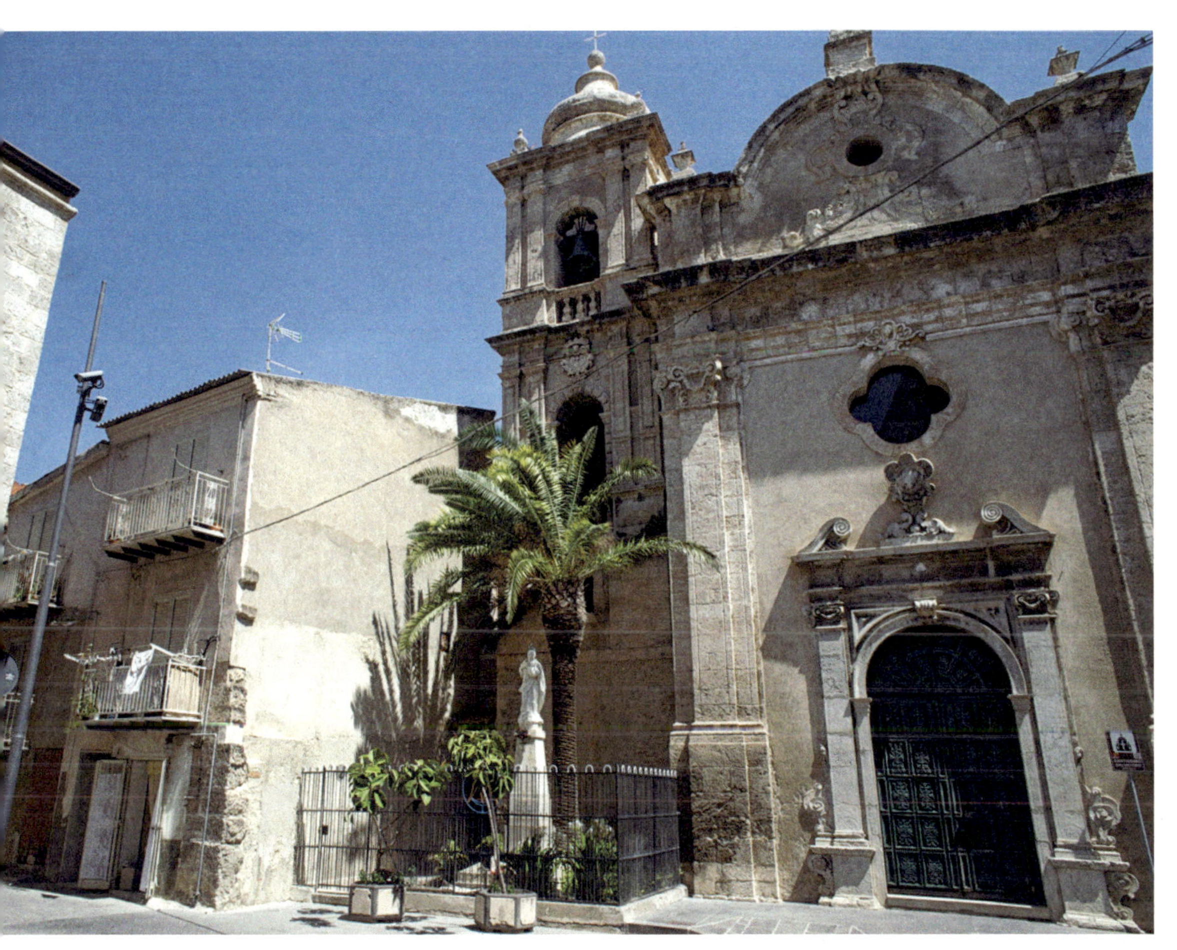

Italy

Landschaft Series (2015–)

Images on the following pages

Landschaft (St. Martin sous Vigouroux, August 26, 11:35 a.m.–12:40 p.m.)
Landschaft (Rouen Cathedral, (side garden) (slightly different position), August 22, 3:15 p.m.–4:15 p.m.)
Landschaft (Rouen Cathedral, (side garden), August 22, 6:00 p.m.)
Landschaft (Rouen Cathedral, August 23, 10:50 a.m.–12:05 p.m.)
Landschaft (Rooftop, Fez Morocco, September 19, 5:10a.m.–6:00 a.m.)
Landschaft (Angel's Gate Park, San Pedro, September 16, 9:00 a.m.)
Landschaft (Piazza Progresso, Licata, Sicily, August 29, 16:10–17:00 p.m.)
Landschaft (At a garden to the side of the Rouen Cathedral, France, August 23, 06:55–08:00 a.m.)
Landschaft (Peter and Paul Cathedral, St. Petersburg, Russia, August 31, 14:45–16:00 p.m.)
Landschaft (*La cloche magique* de Vigouroux, Cantal, France, August 24, 11:15–11:45 a.m.)

All images: watercolour, colour pencil, pencil, ink, stamp on paper; 18.6 x 27.5 cm

Drawings in the "Landschaft" series are "soundscape sketches." These sketches were created on the road, so the choice of medium was born out of a practical consideration. I used only materials that were easy to bring with me when traveling.

I started making these images as experiments, to give myself something to do when I was waiting for the various bells to ring. Sound sketches of landscapes have since become an important part of my practice.

Consider a landscape painting: Temporality in landscape painting is somewhat concealed; it is presented to us as a snapshot of a single moment, as in the case of landscape photography. To paint a landscape is in fact to flatten time. In my sound sketches, the passing of time as an integral aspect of a landscape is always at the forefront.

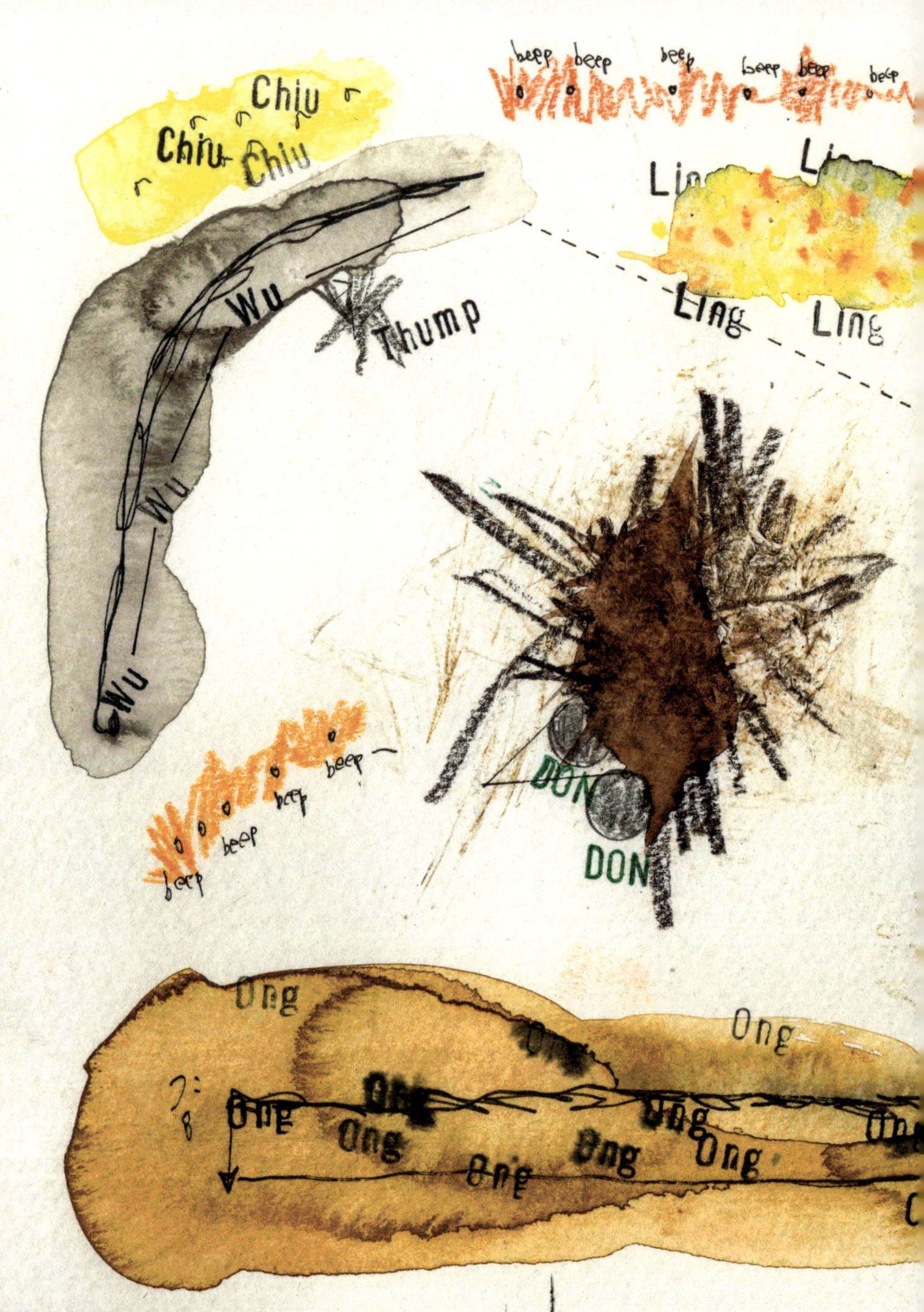
Chiu
Chiu Chiu
beep beep beep beep beep beep
Ling
Ling
Ling Ling
Wu
Thump
Wu
Wu
Wu
beep
beep
beep
beep
beep
DON
DON
Ong
Ong
Ong
Ong
Ong
Ong
Ong
Ong
Ong
Ong

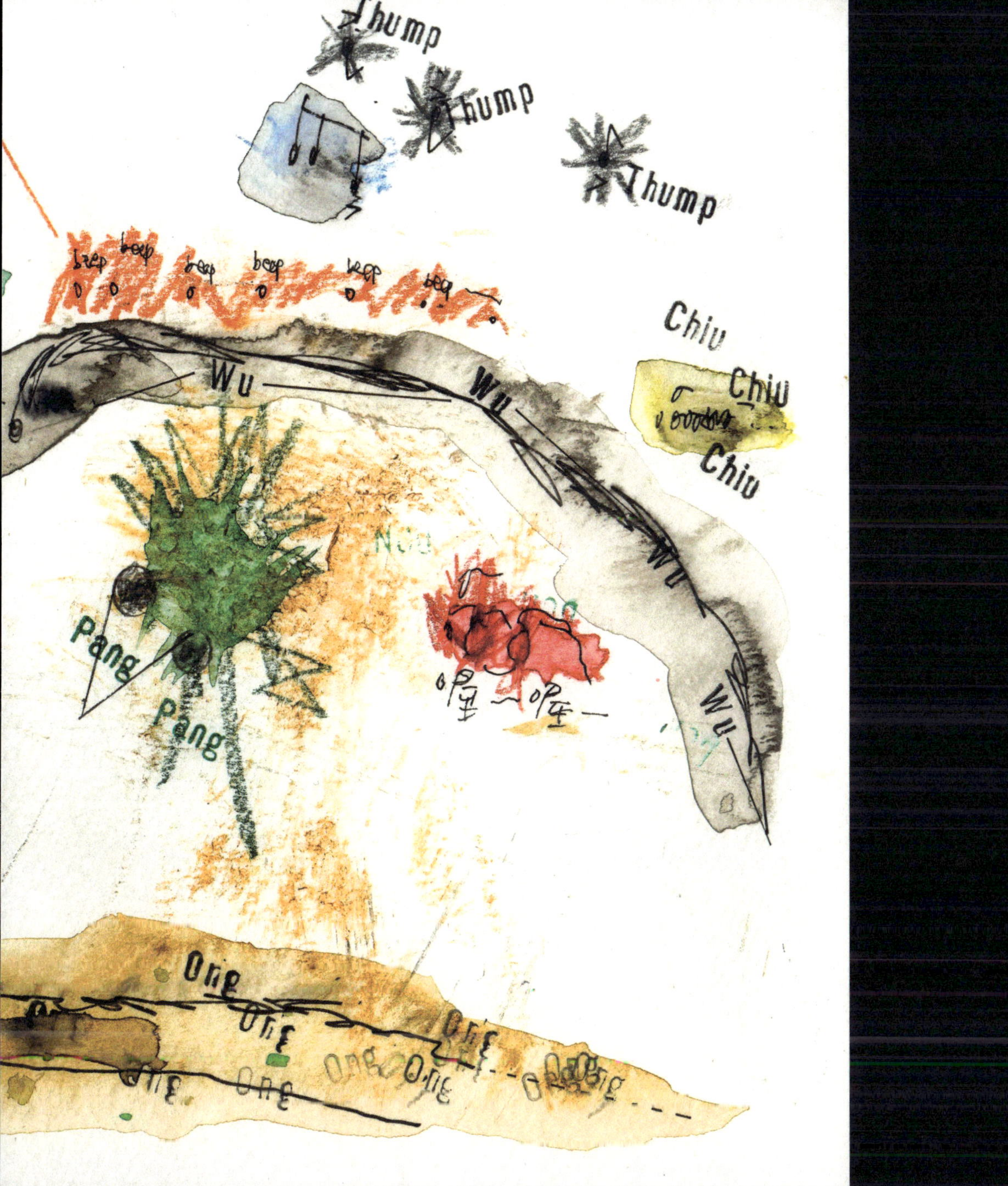

Thump
Thump
Thump
beep beep beep beep beep beep
Chiu
Chiu
Chiu
Wu
Wu
Wu
Wu
Pang
Pang
One
One
One
One
One
One
One
One

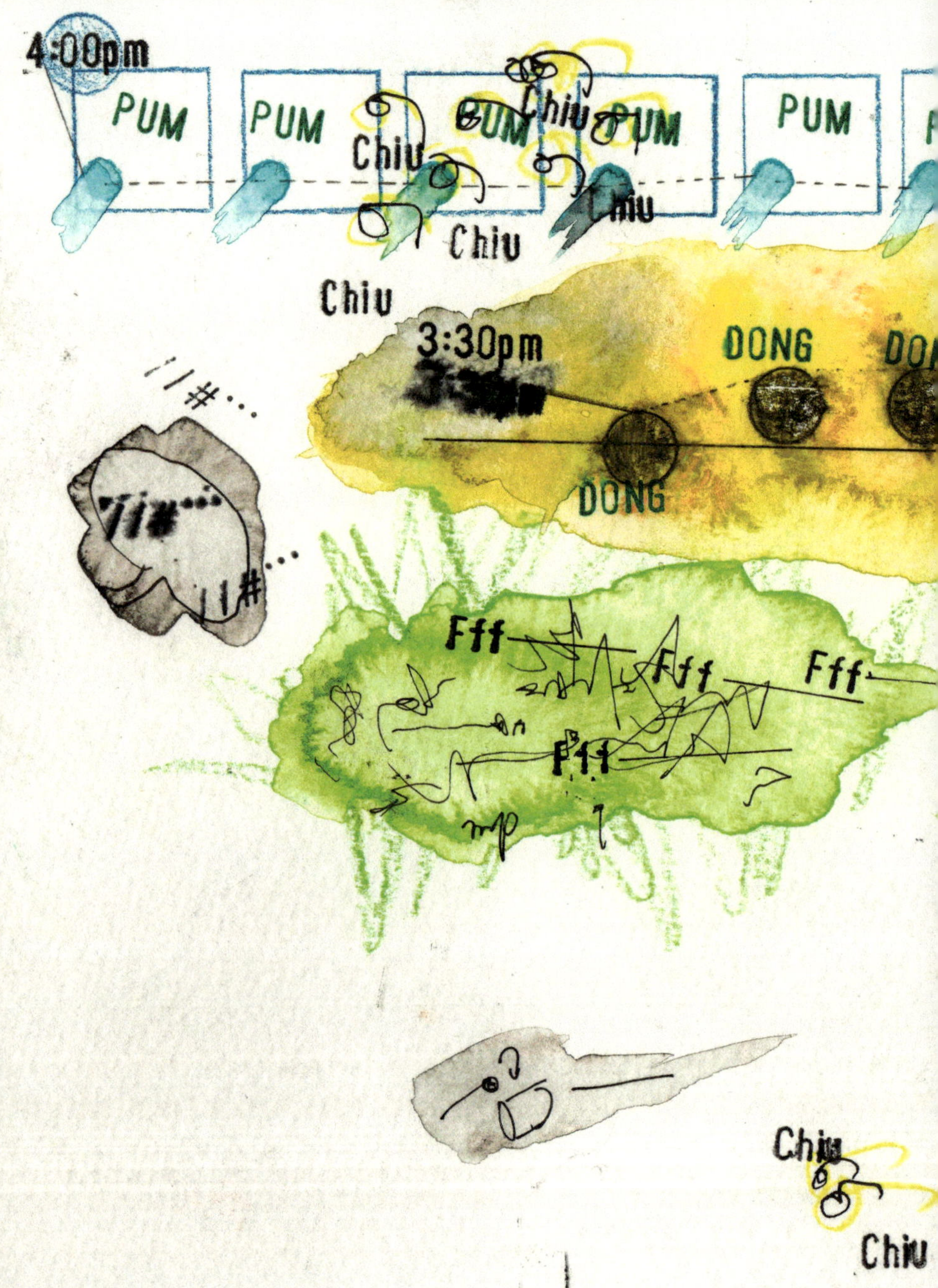
4:00pm
PUM
PUM
PUM
PUM
PUM
Chiu
Chiu
Chiu
Chiu
Chiu
3:30pm
DONG
DONG
DONG
DONG
Fff
Fff
Fff
Fff
Chiu
Chiu

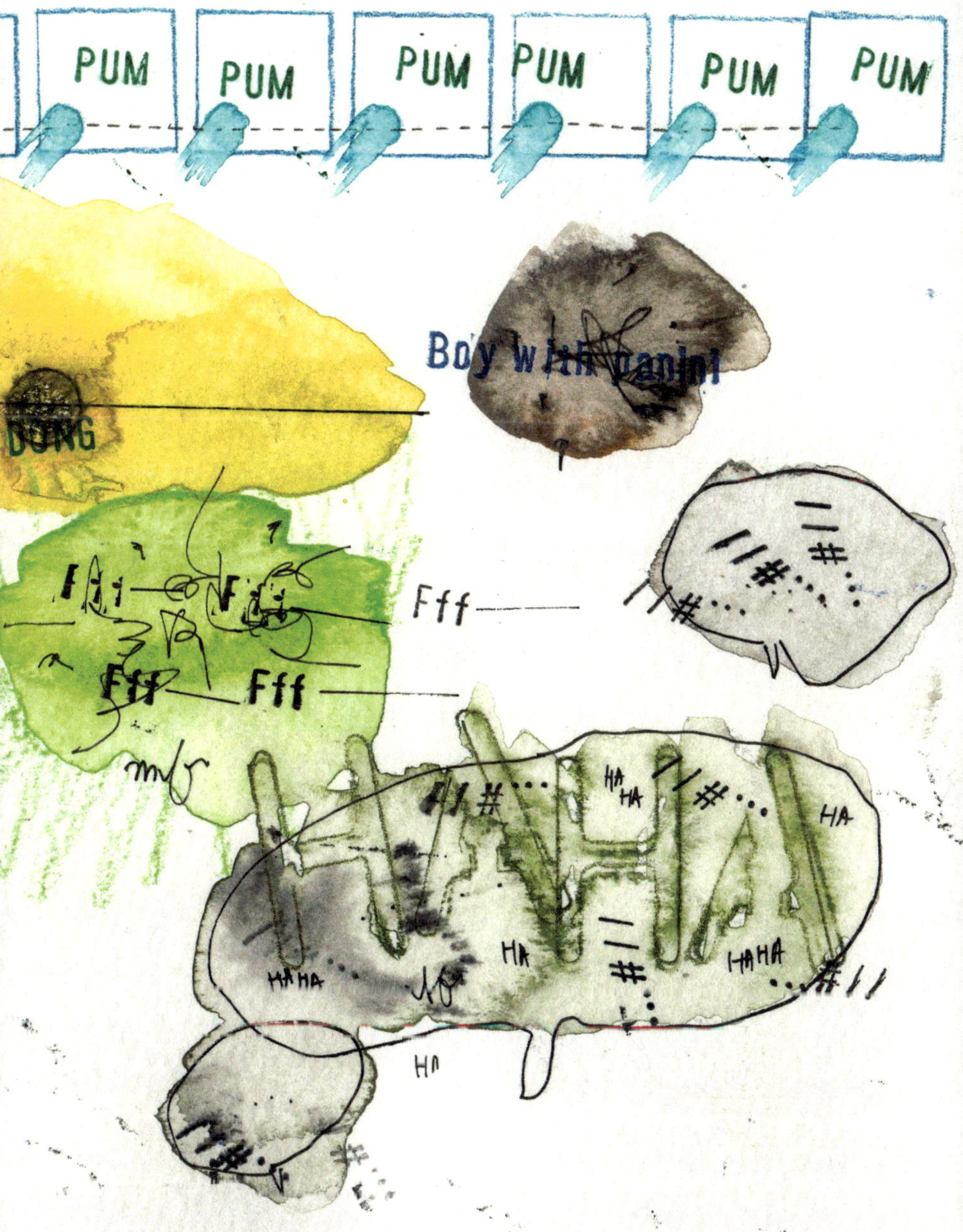

PUM PUM PUM PUM PUM PUM PUM
Boy with panini
DONG
Fff
Fff
Fff Fff
mf
HAHA
HA
HA
HA
HAHA
HAHA

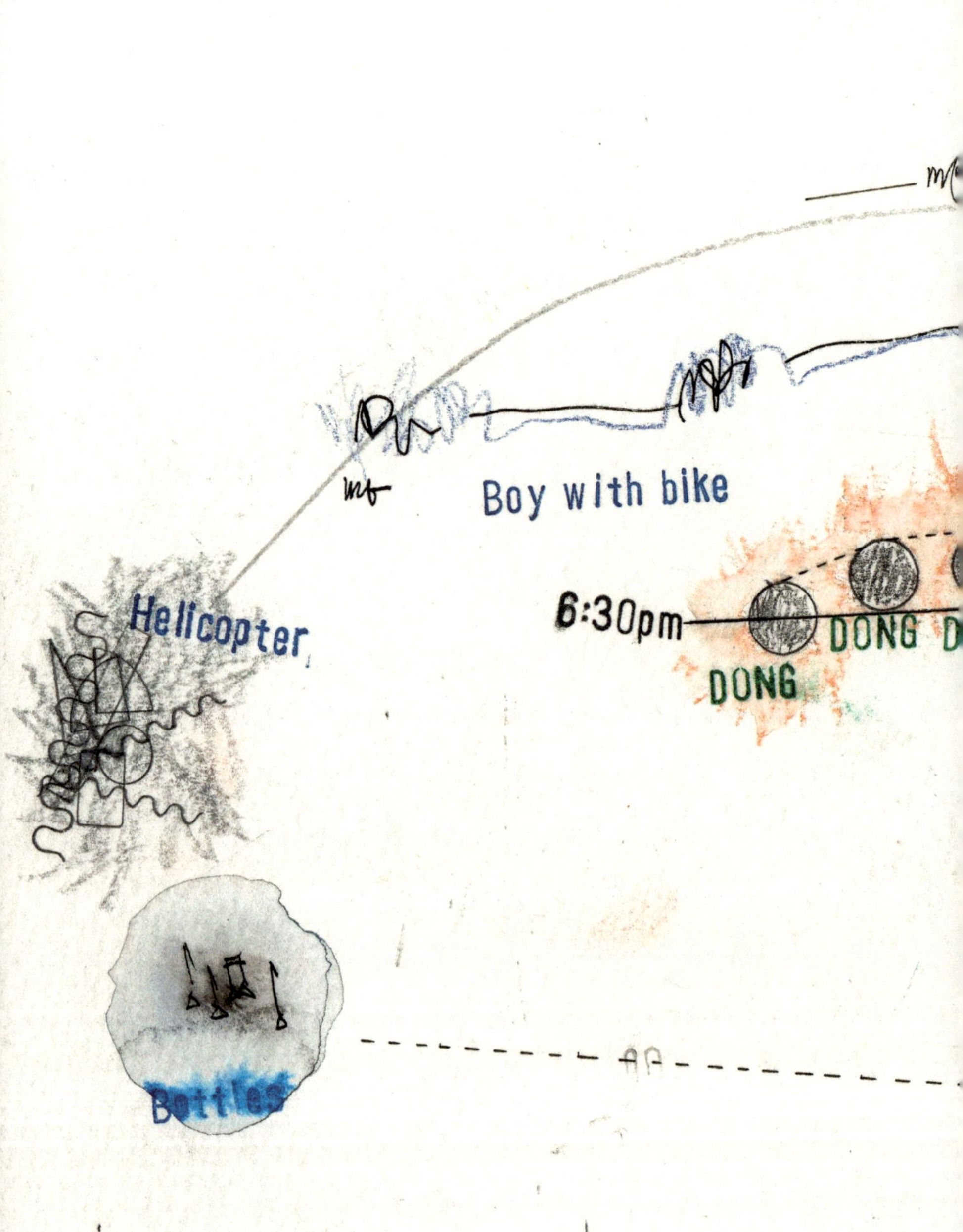
Boy with bike
Helicopter
6:30pm
DONG DONG
DONG
Bottles

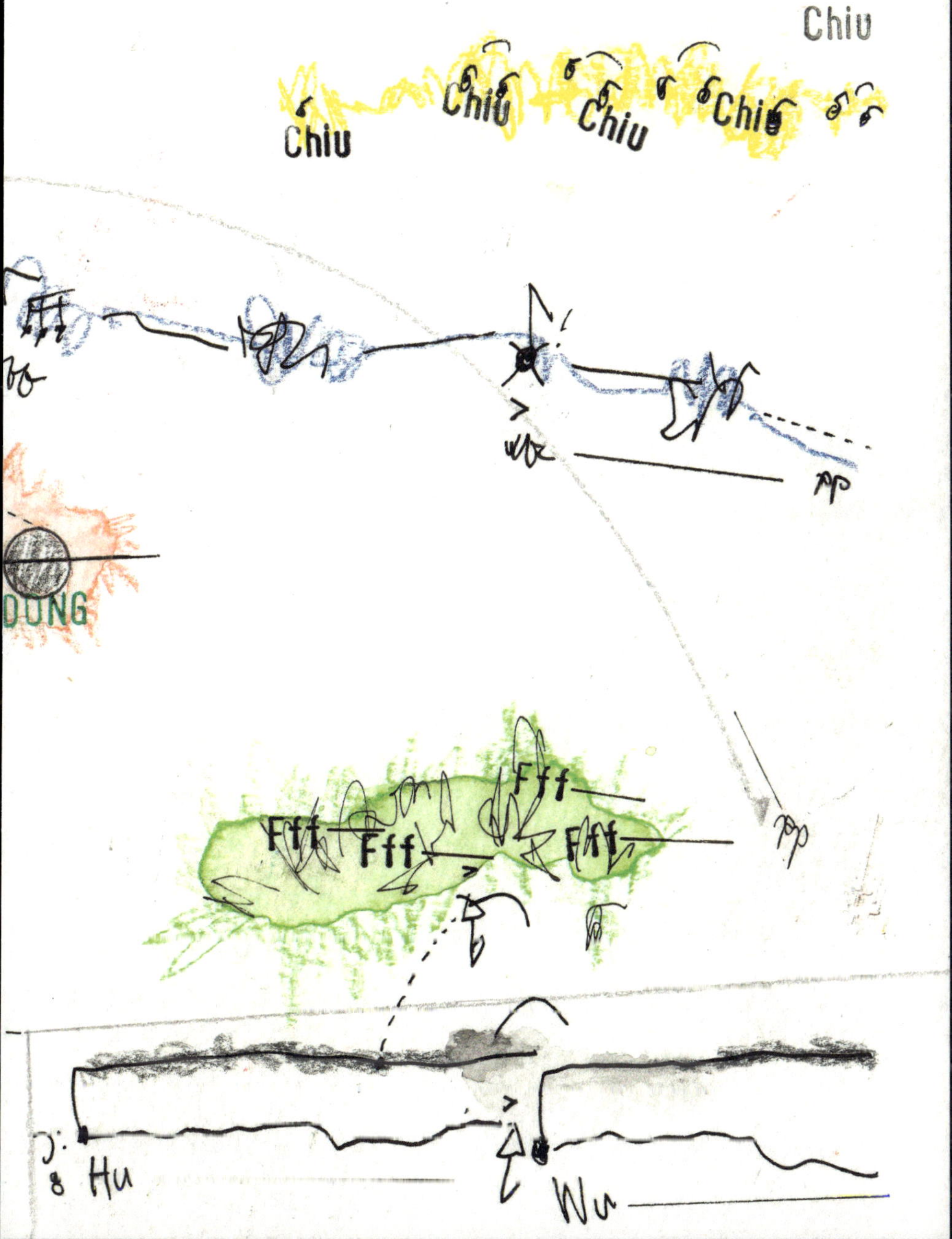

Chiu

Chiu Chiu Chiu Chie

DOONG

Fff Fff Fff Fff

pp

pp

Hu

Wu

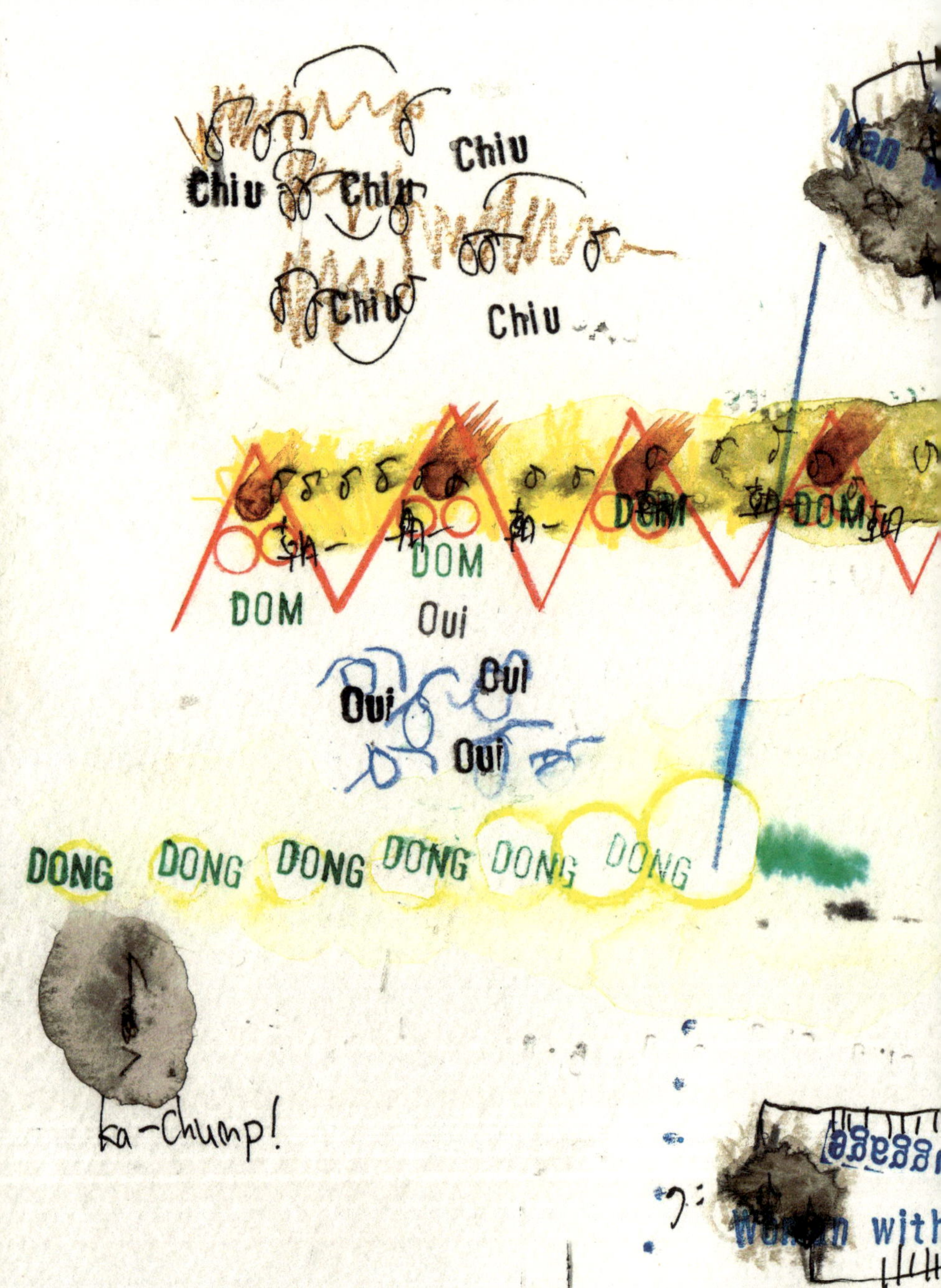

Chiu
Chiu
Chiu
Chiu
Chiu
Chiu
Man
DOM
DOM
DOM
DOM
Oui
Oui
Oui
Oui
Oui
DONG DONG DONG DONG DONG DONG DONG
ka-Chump!
Woman with

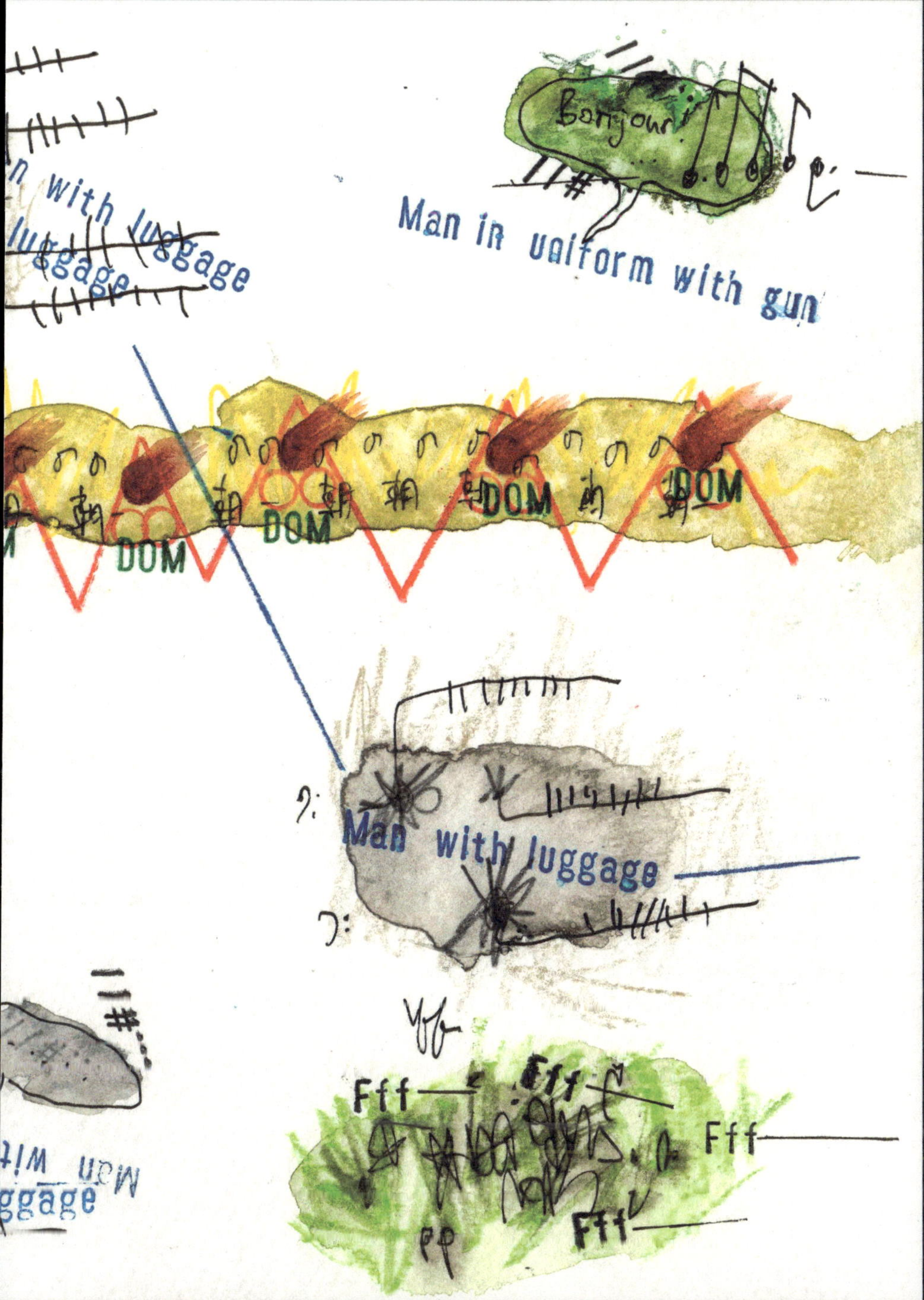

with luggage
luggage

Bonjour

Man in uniform with gun

DOM DOM DOM DOM

Man with luggage

Man wit... luggage

Fff Fff Fff

pp

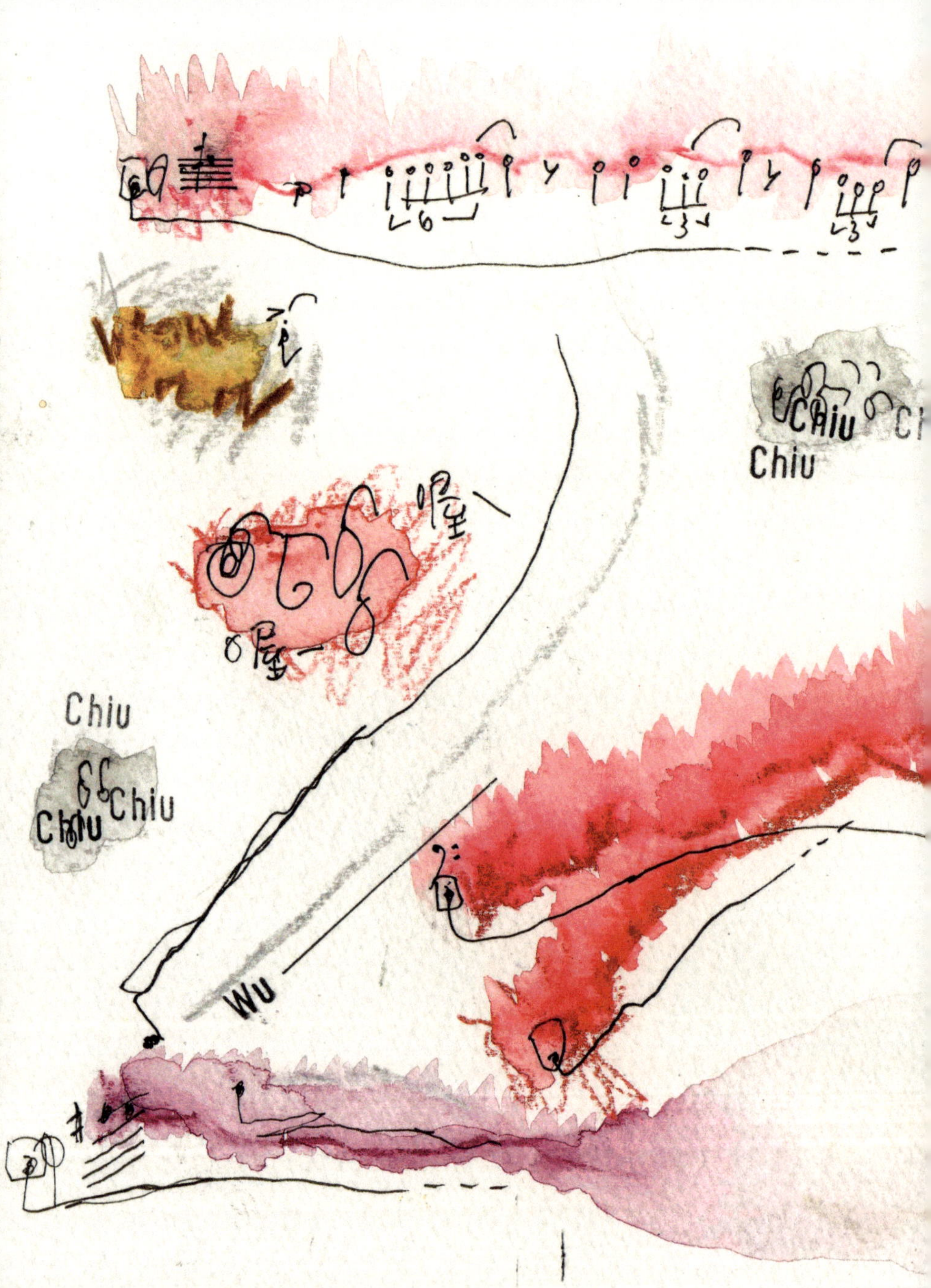

Chiu
Chiu
Chiu
Chiu
Chiu
Wu

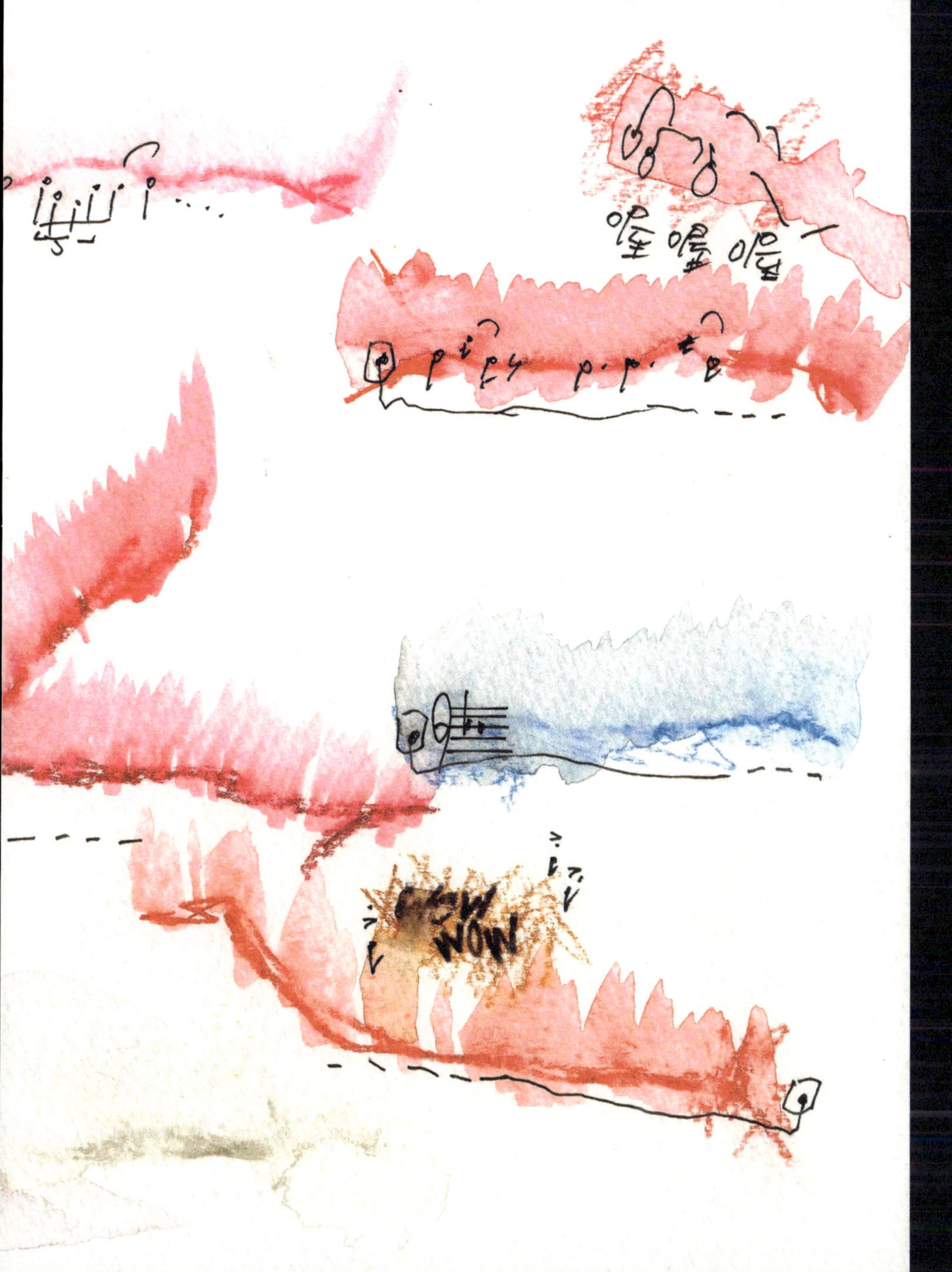
아돌 아돌 아돌
WOW

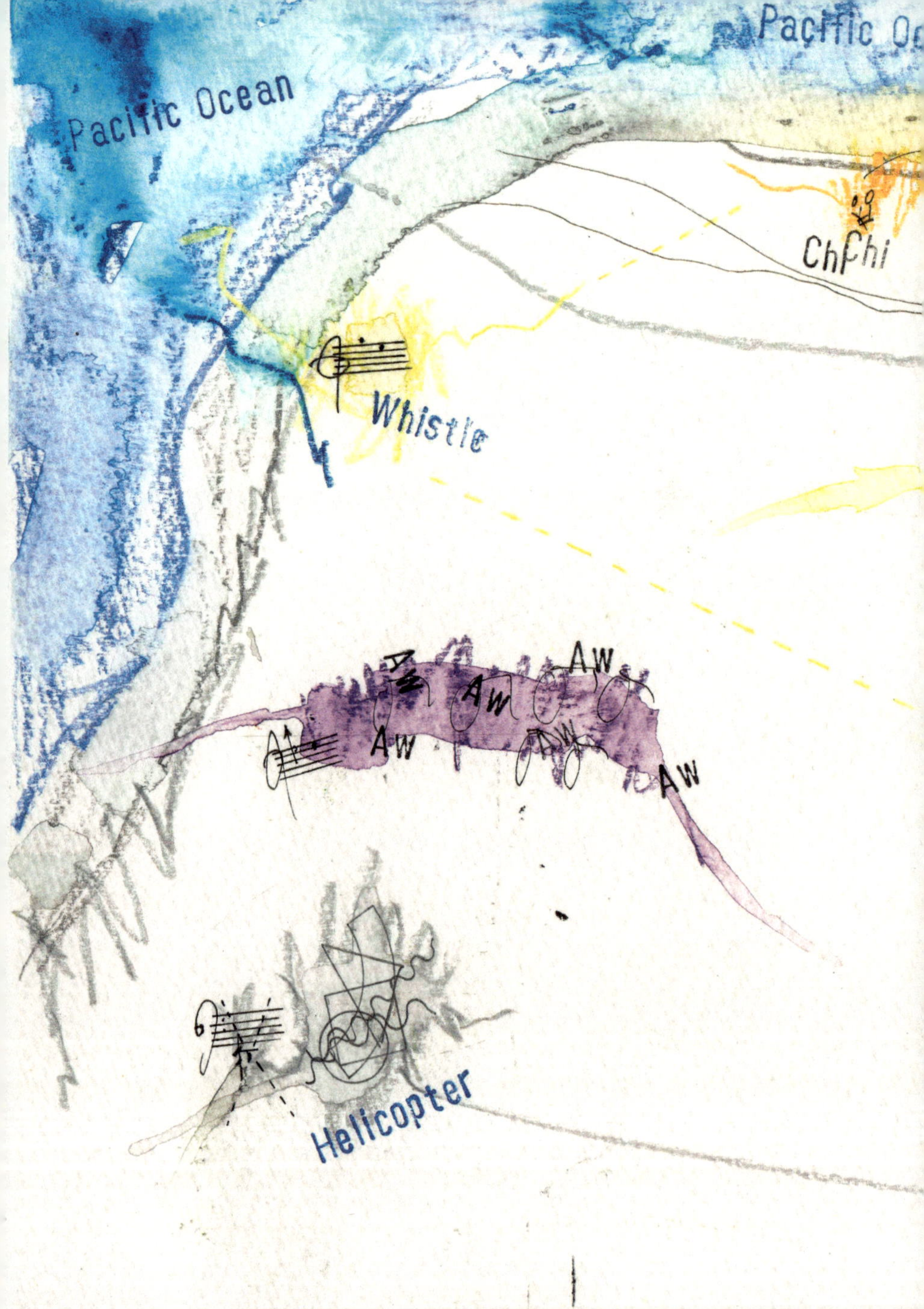

Pacific Ocean
Pacific O
ChFhi
Whistle
Aw
Aw
Aw
Aw
Aw
Aw
Helicopter

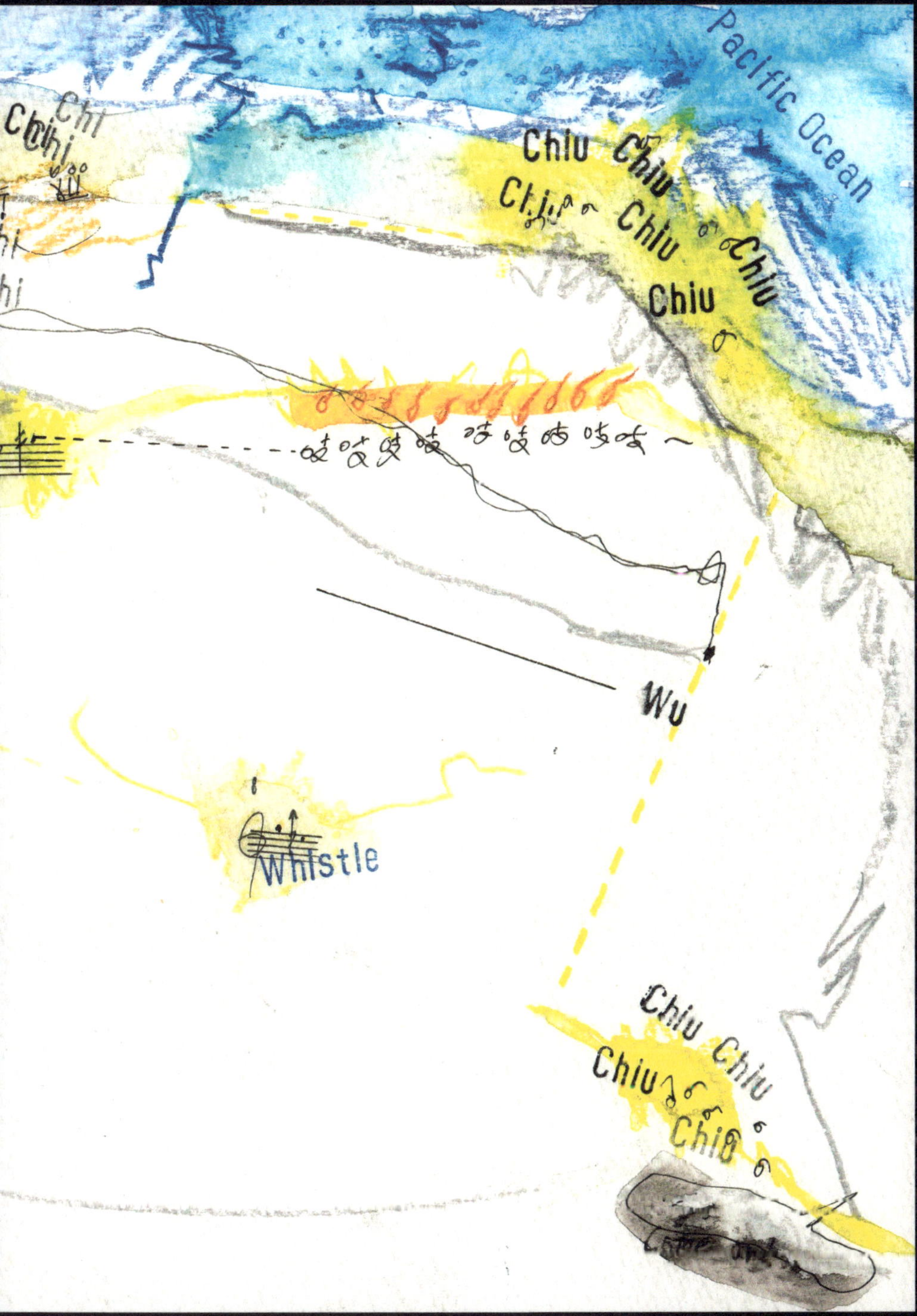

Pacific Ocean
Chi
Chichi
Chiu Chiu
Chiu Chiu
Chiu Chiu
Chiu
Wu
Whistle
Chiu Chiu
Chiu Chiu
Chiu

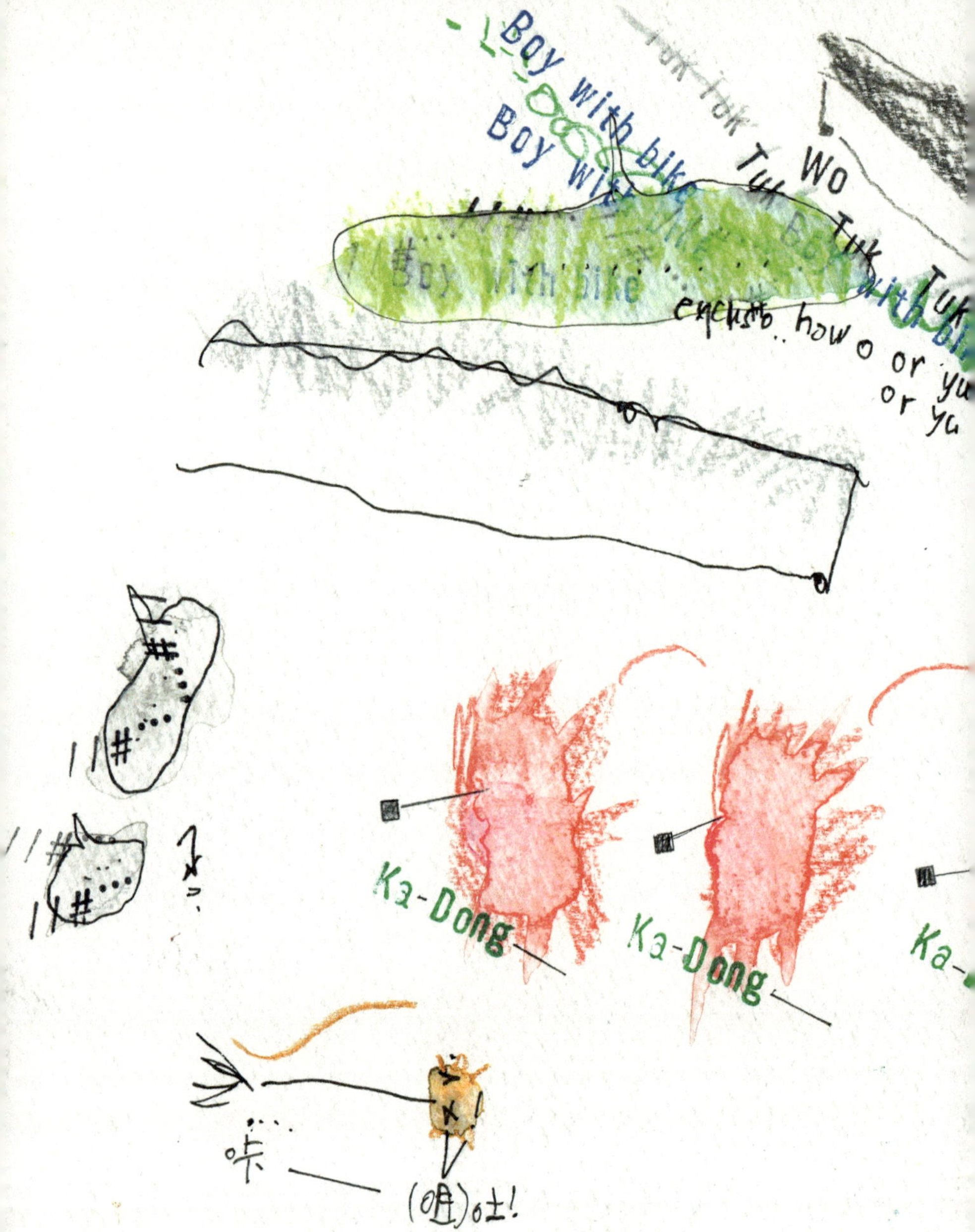

Boy with bike
Dog
Boy with bike
Boy with bike
Tuk-Tuk Tuk Tuk Tuk
WO Tuk Tuk Tuk
excuse.. how o or yu
or yu

Ka-Dong   Ka-Dong   Ka-

咔

(咖)吐!

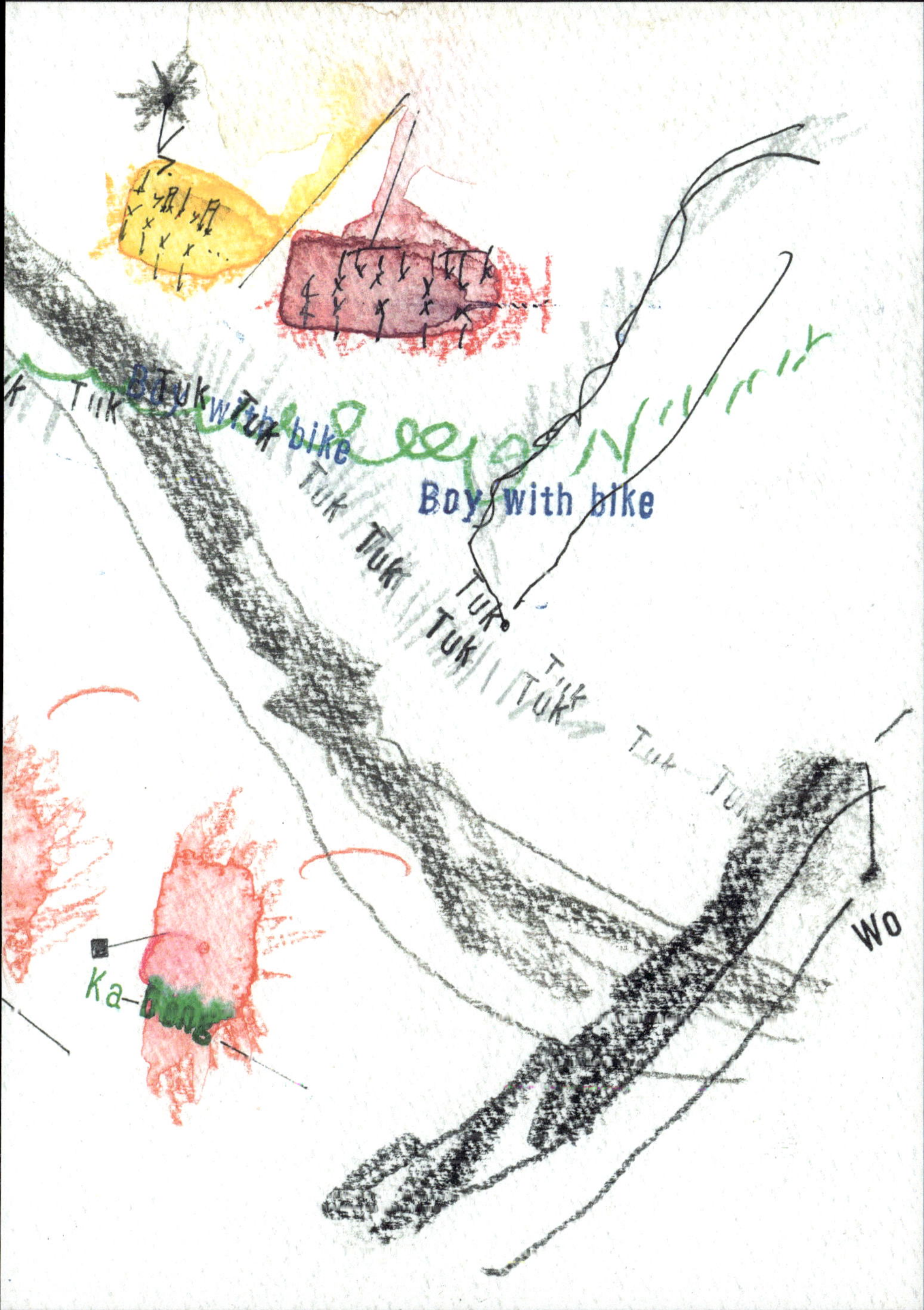

Tuk Tuk Boy with bike Tuk Tuk Tuk Tuk Tuk Tuk Tuk Tuk

Boy with bike

Ka-Bong

Wo

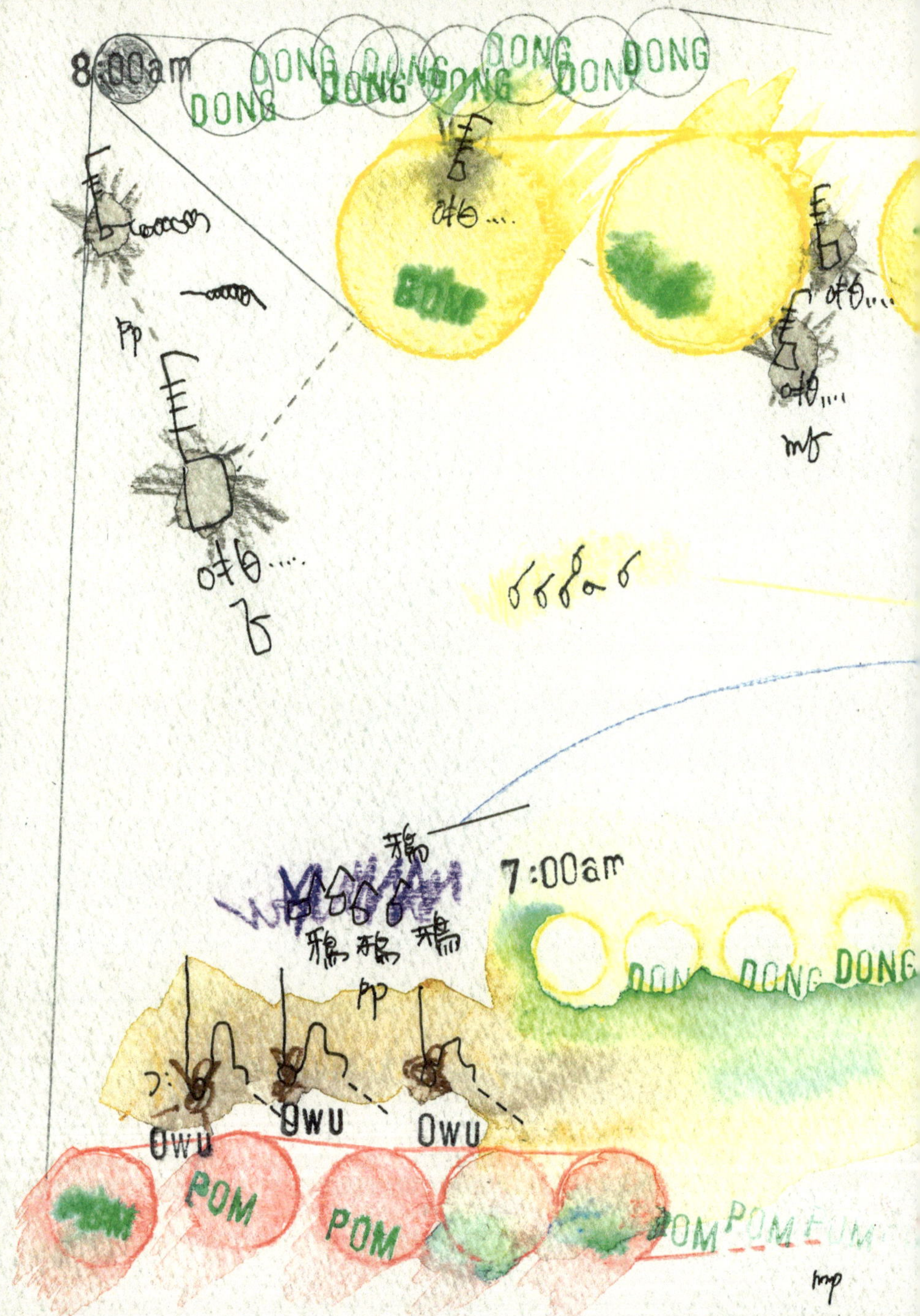

8:00am
DONG DONG DONG DONG DONG DONG DONG DONG
BOM
7:00am
DONG DONG DONG
OWU OWU OWU
POM POM POM POM POM EOM

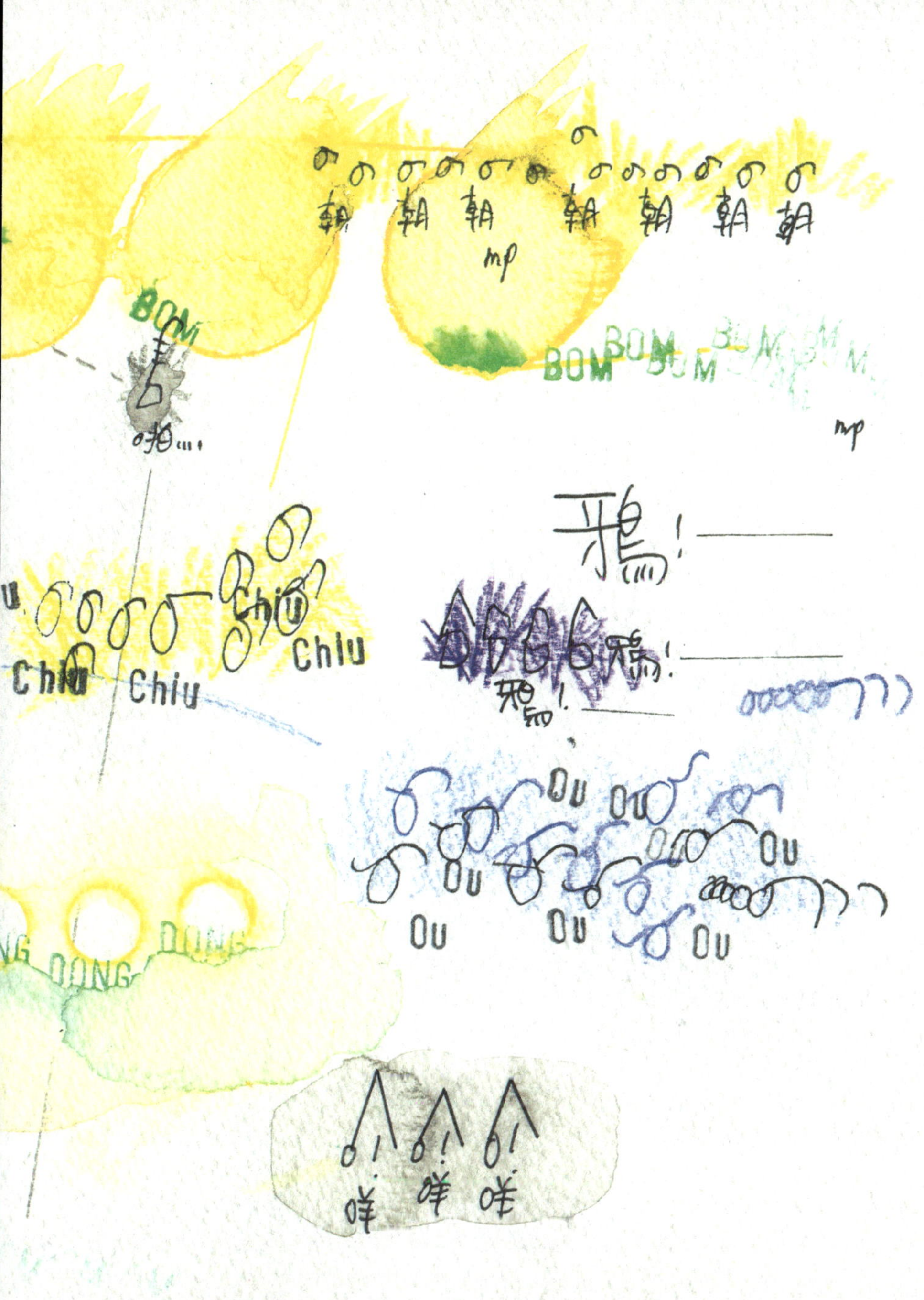
mp
朝 朝 朝 朝 朝 朝 朝
BOM
BOM BOM BOM BOM
mp
Chiu Chiu Chiu Chiu
u
鵝!
鵝!
鵝!
OU OU OU
OU OU
OU OU OU
DONG DONG
咩 咩 咩

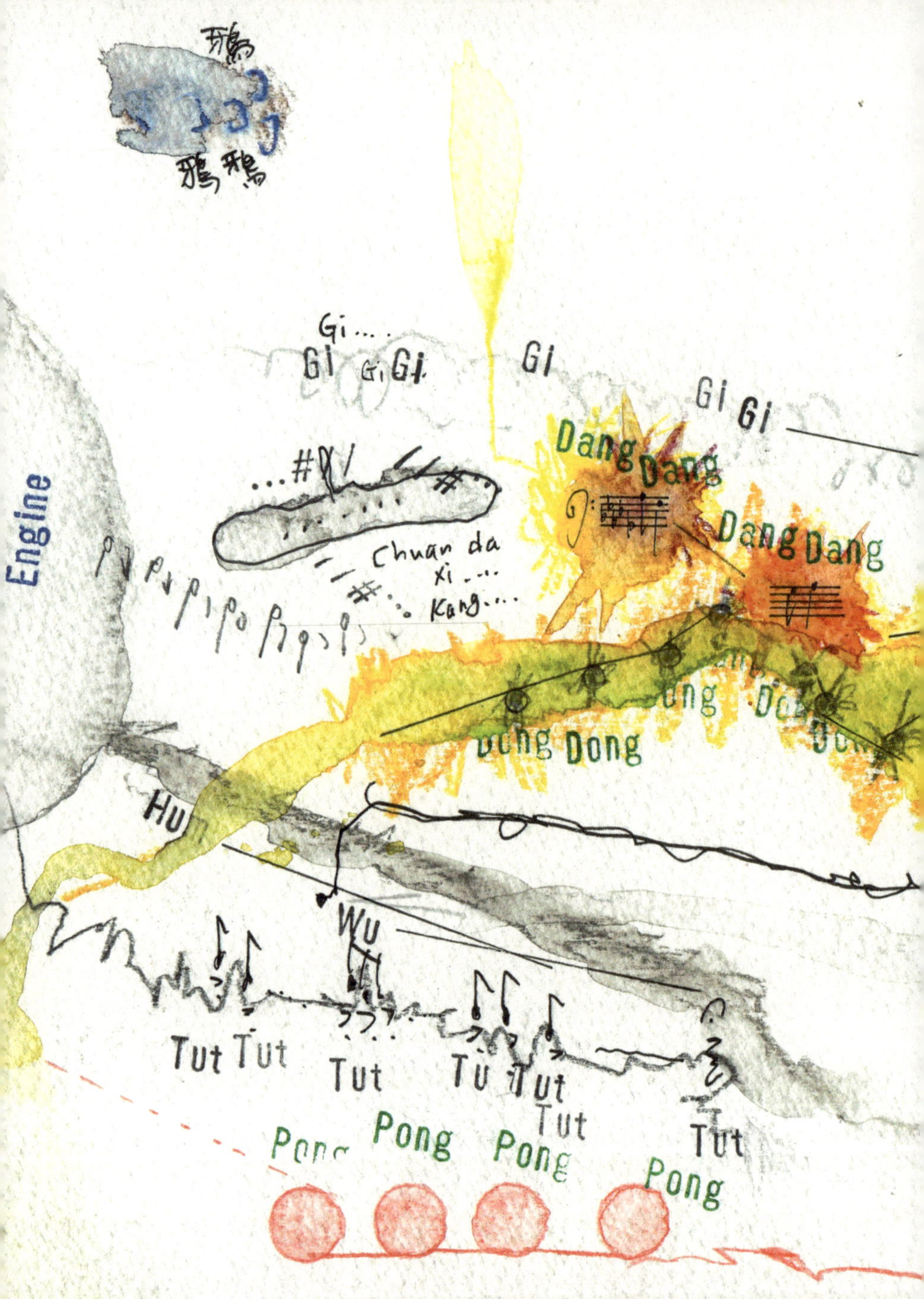

Engine
Gi....
Gi Gi Gi.
Gi
Gi Gi
...#
Chuan da
xi....
Kang....
Dang Dang
Dang Dang
Dong Dong
Hu
Wu
Tut Tut
Tut
Tut Tut
Tut
Tut
Pong Pong Pong
Pong

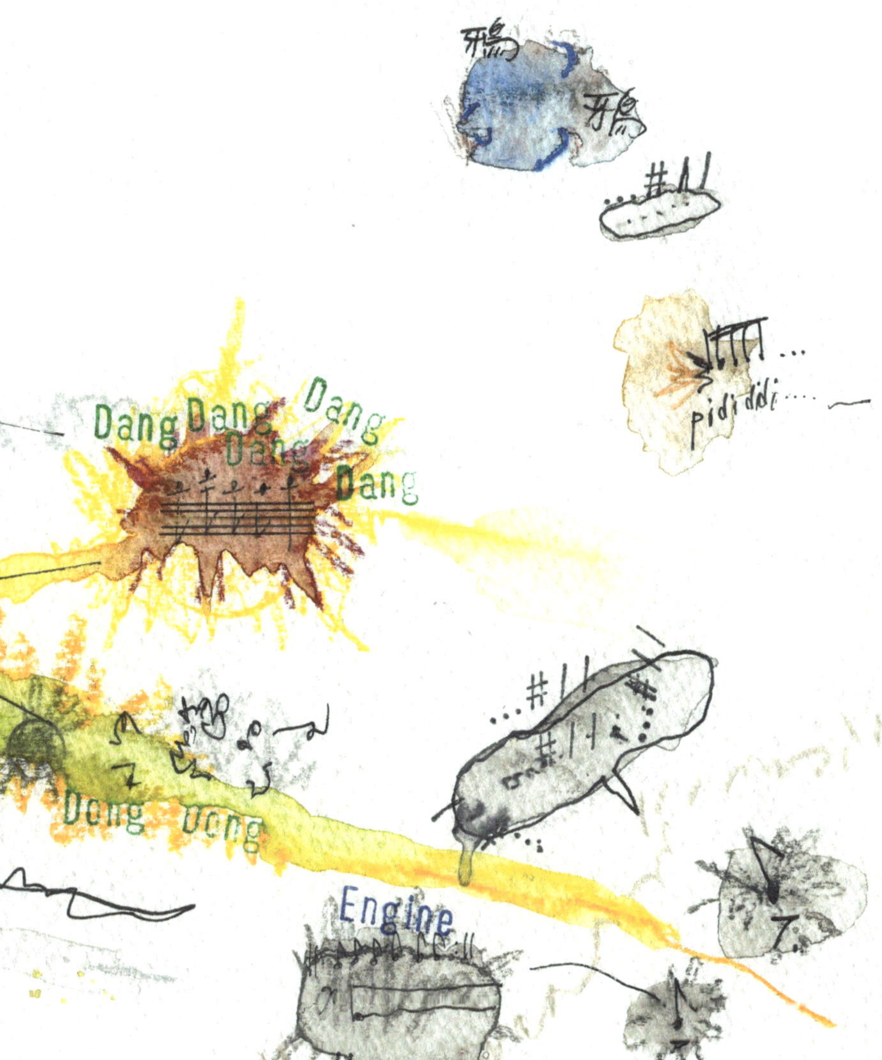

Dang Dang Dang
Dang
Dang
Dang Dong
pididi
Engine
Um

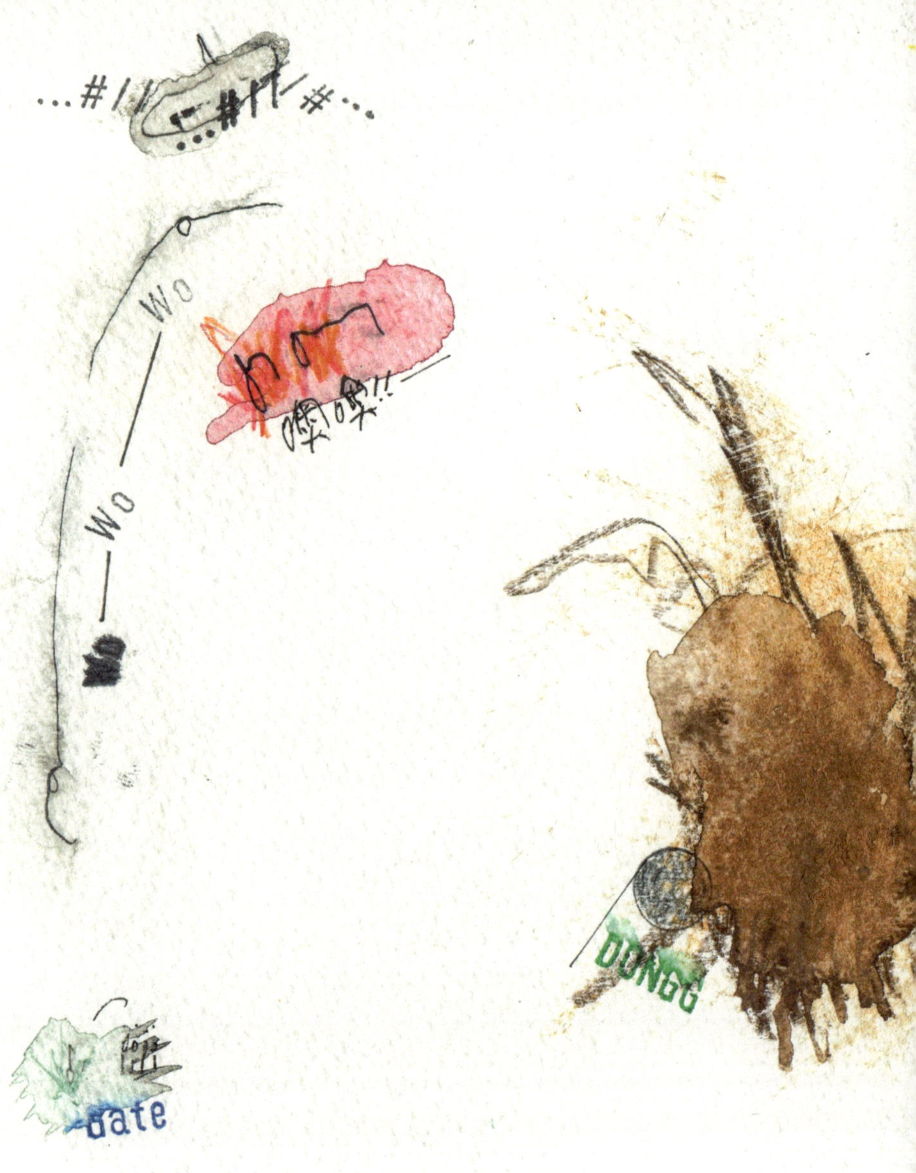
...#///#/#/#...
Wo
Wo
Date
DONGG

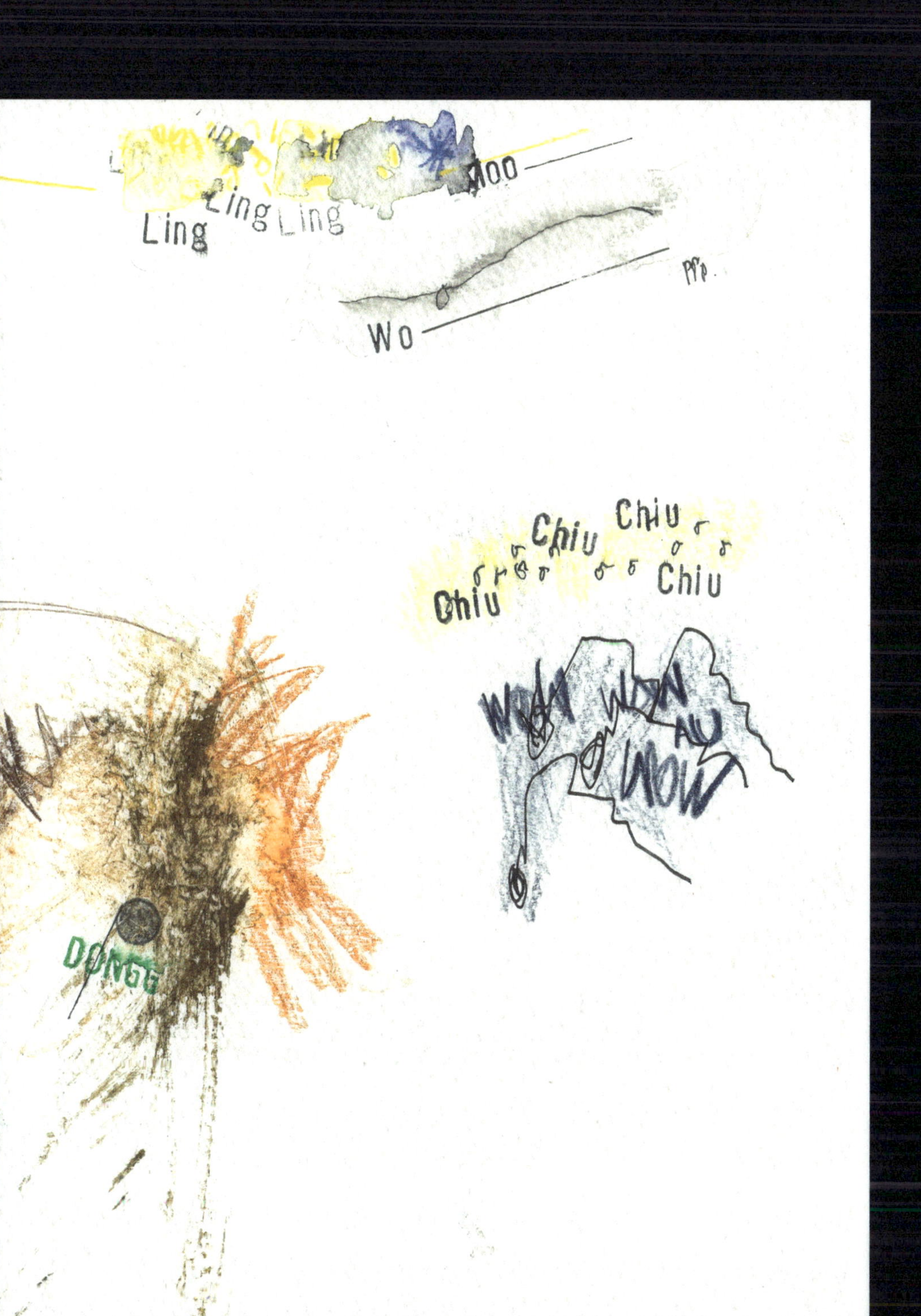

Ling
Ling Ling
Moo
Wo
ppp.
Chiu
Chiu
Chiu
Chiu
DONGG

Russia

My purpose in visiting St. Petersburg was both single-minded and something of a mission impossible: to make a clean recording of the bells of the Great Peacock Clock. Through the good folks at BMW, I submitted a pretty ridiculous request to the Hermitage: I asked the museum to allow me to record the clock in solitude outside the museum's opening hours. The museum receives upward of two million visitors per year. The Great Peacock Clock is one of the most valuable gems of the institution and the Russian people. There were some initial positive responses, but I harbored no hope. Nonetheless, a couple of days before I was due in the city, the museum gave the green light. I was instructed to arrive at the back entrance of the Hermitage fifteen minutes before the museum would be closed to the public. It was one of the most remarkable things to have happened to me on what was already an unbelievably rich journey.

The Great Peacock Clock inhabits the dining room where Catherine the Great received her closest military allies and friends. The bird, glittering with gold and precious stones, is a sight to behold. It was the creation of British jeweler James Cox, and arguably his finest. It is musical automaton, luxury timepiece, sound installation, and robotic art all coming together in a beautiful sculptural object.

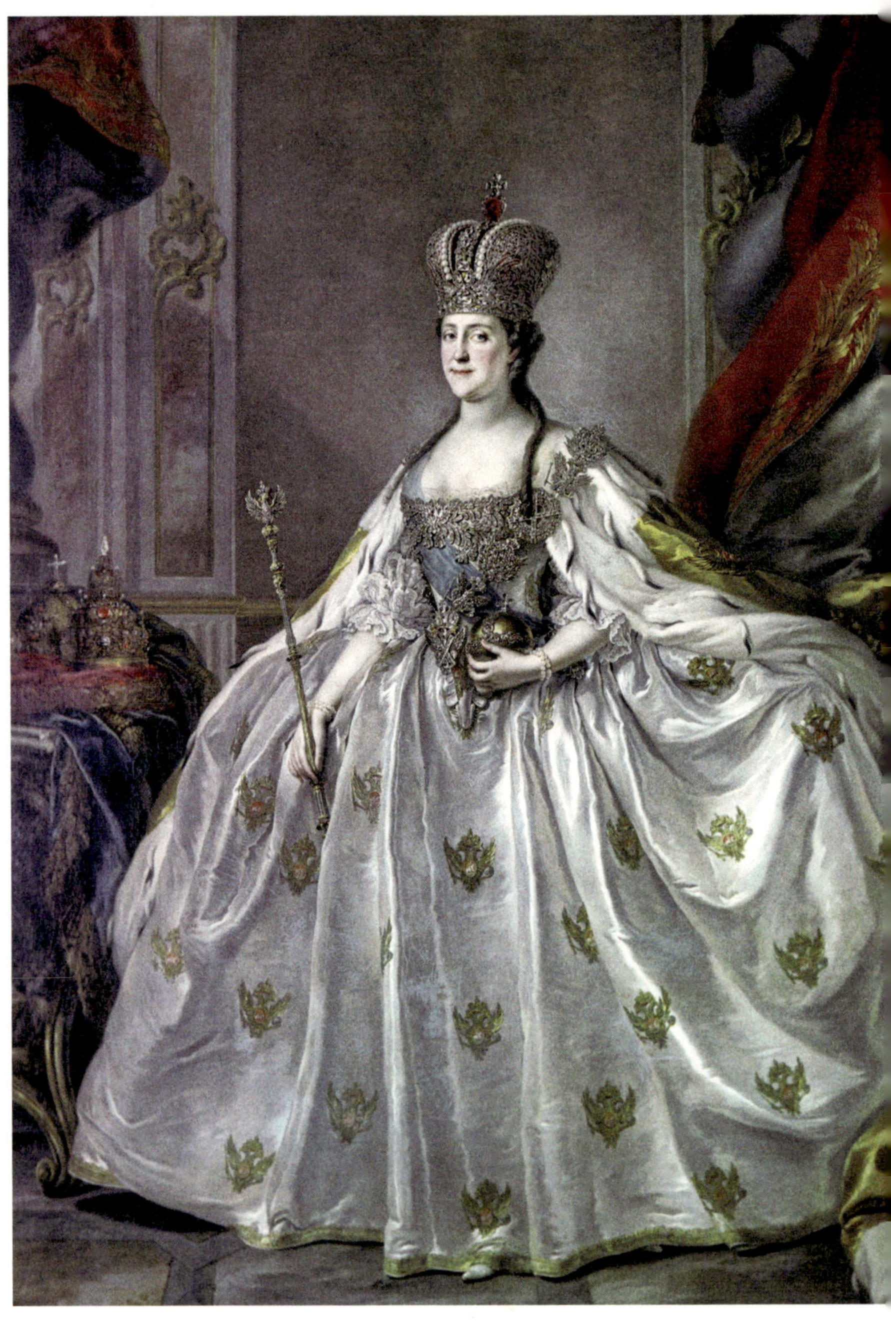

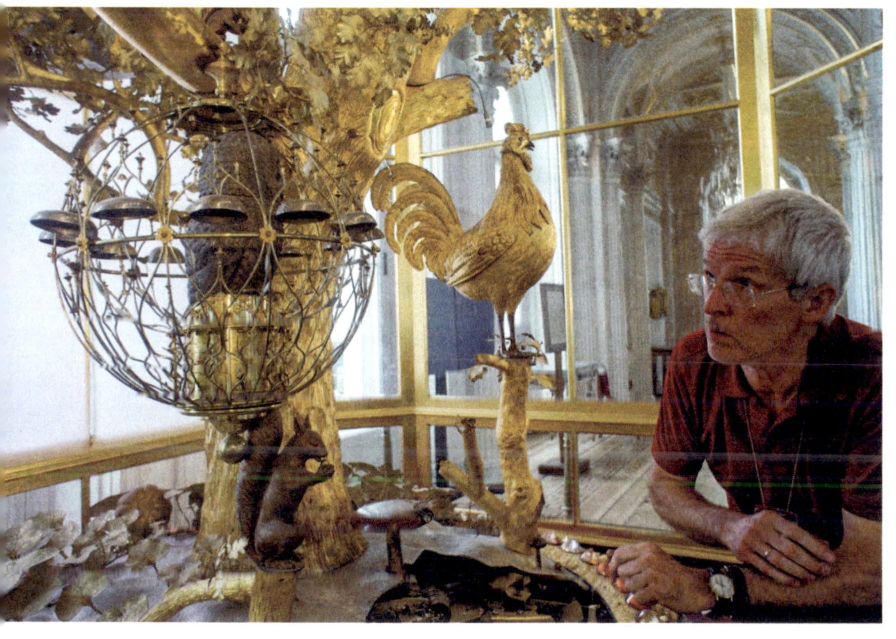

Russia

It was also General Potemkin's gift of love to Catherine at the height of their passionate and politically charged relationship.

Upon arrival at the Hermitage, I was greeted by Viktor Korobov, the museum's head of restoration (who apparently is the only person in the institution allowed to touch the peacock). Viktor carefully unlocked the peacock's cage. I stepped inside and knelt underneath its wings. I was so taken that I involuntarily held my breath for a moment. Viktor proceeded to crank the clock to just before the hour, and the peacock began to make the most amazing noises. When it's heard from up close, there is a cacophony of mechanical and musical sounds—not always harmonious, often aggressive, but always rich in dissonances and contradictions. It occurred to me that in the pre-recording age, the Great Peacock Clock must have been the thing of myths and legends.

We are severely deprived when it comes to vocabularies to represent sounds. How does one describe a sound without naming its origin? (Many sound artists have already noted that the English language is notoriously bad in this regard; Chinese is perhaps a little better, but that's another story.) The peacock's performance ended in a melodic quarter-hour chime, which I later discovered is exactly

the same as the quarter-hour chime at the Peter and Paul
Cathedral, where Catherine was buried. Something that
should have been obvious but that I learned anew on this
trip: Devotion produces the most beautiful art.

We are incredibly good at inventing metaphors for things
that elude description. I still don't understand why the
people of nineteenth-century rural France cared so much
about thunderstorms, but ever since Cantal, I have been
thinking about the literary soundscape of a "sweet thunder"
from the first scene of *A Midsummer Night's Dream:*

> Hippolyta: … Never did I hear
> Such gallant chiding: for, besides the groves,
> The skies, the fountains, every region near
> Seem'd all one mutual cry: I never heard
> So musical a discord, Such Sweet Thunder.

The composition that this journey will produce is slowly
taking shape in my head. I will probably call the piece
Such Sweet Thunder.

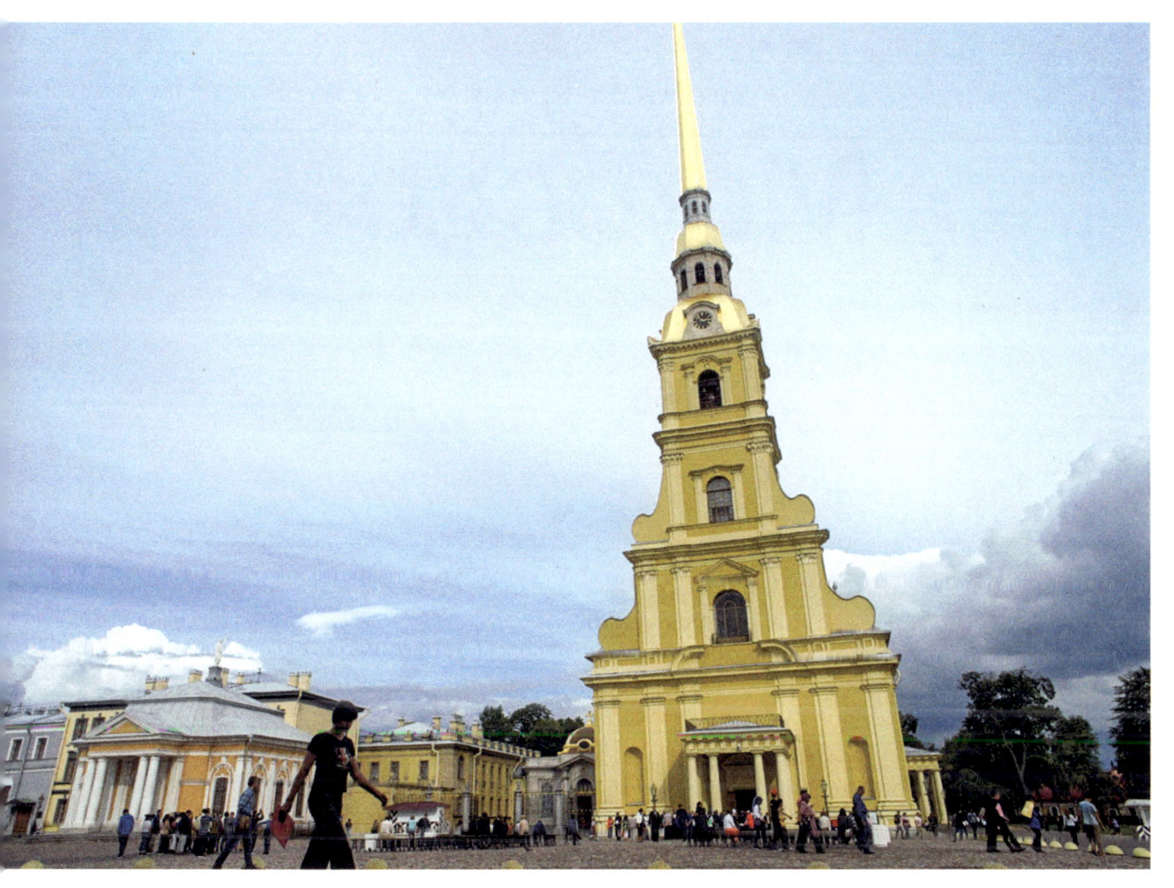

Morocco

Fez is an assault on the senses.

From my observations, contemporary political discourse abuses war as a metaphor. The effect is an aura of constant danger, of invisible but ubiquitous foes, an anxiety that results in the relinquishing of the people's power. From George W. Bush's "War on Terror" to China's recent "War on Corruption," we now habitually describe disagreement as combat, and processes of resolution in terms of military strategy. For over a decade now, we have seen how these rhetorical tropes and metaphors often perform the horrific realities they refer to into being.

I came to Fez to visit a "silenced" bell. The bell originally came from the city of Gibraltar, and was war loot of Prince Abu Malik, son of Abu al-Hasan Ali, sultan of Morocco, who conquered the then-Spanish-occupied coastal region in 1333. In the hand of the Marinid king, the bell was transformed into the perfect metaphor for the Islamic world's triumph over Christianity. The bell's tongue was removed. Its body became the core of a chandelier, which was installed at the prayer hall of Al-Qarawiyyin Mosque and Religious College—the world's oldest university. Not only was the musical instrument defaced and silenced, but it became a decorative ornament that emits not sound but flickering light. Today, Al-Qarawiyyin is off-limits

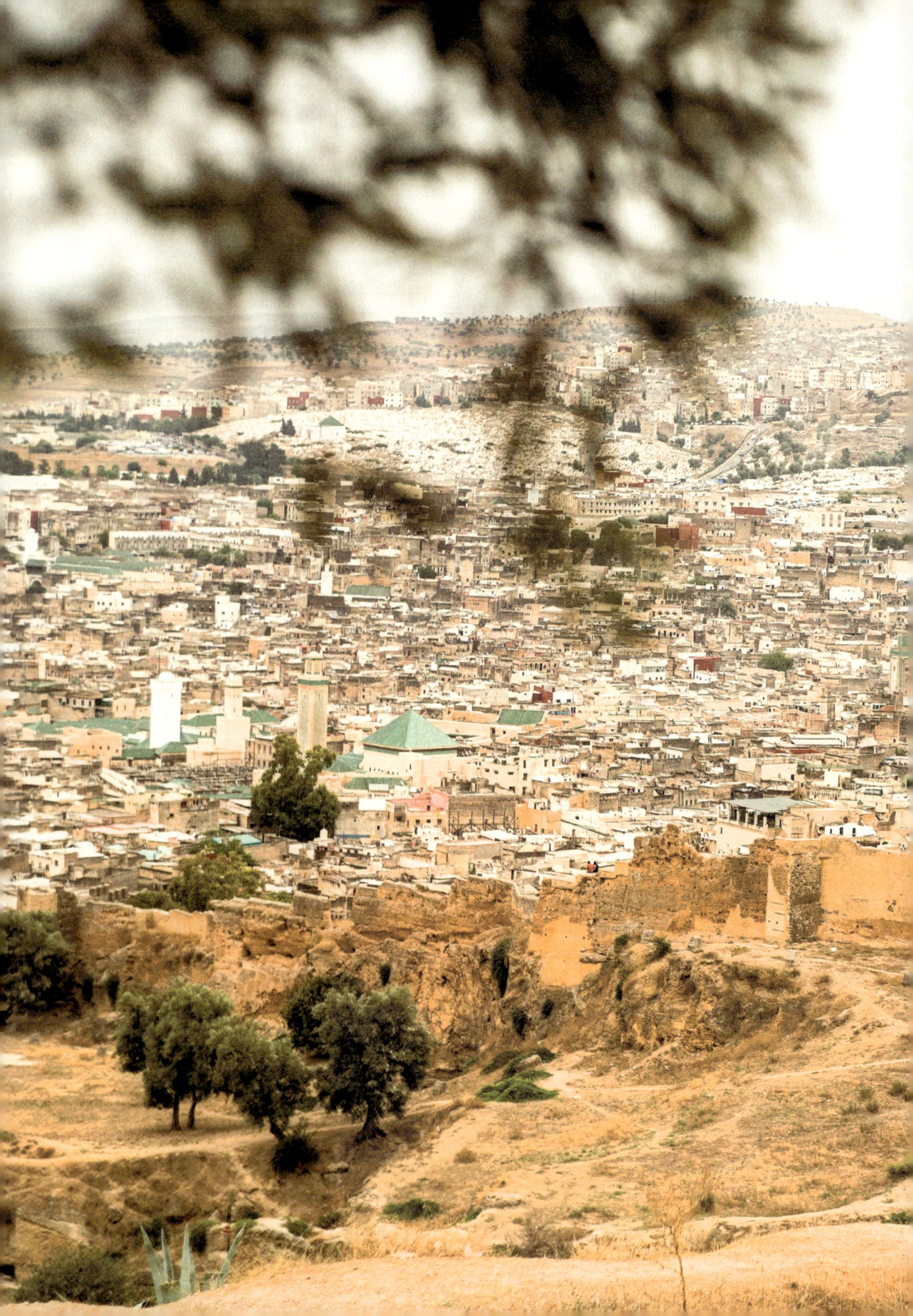

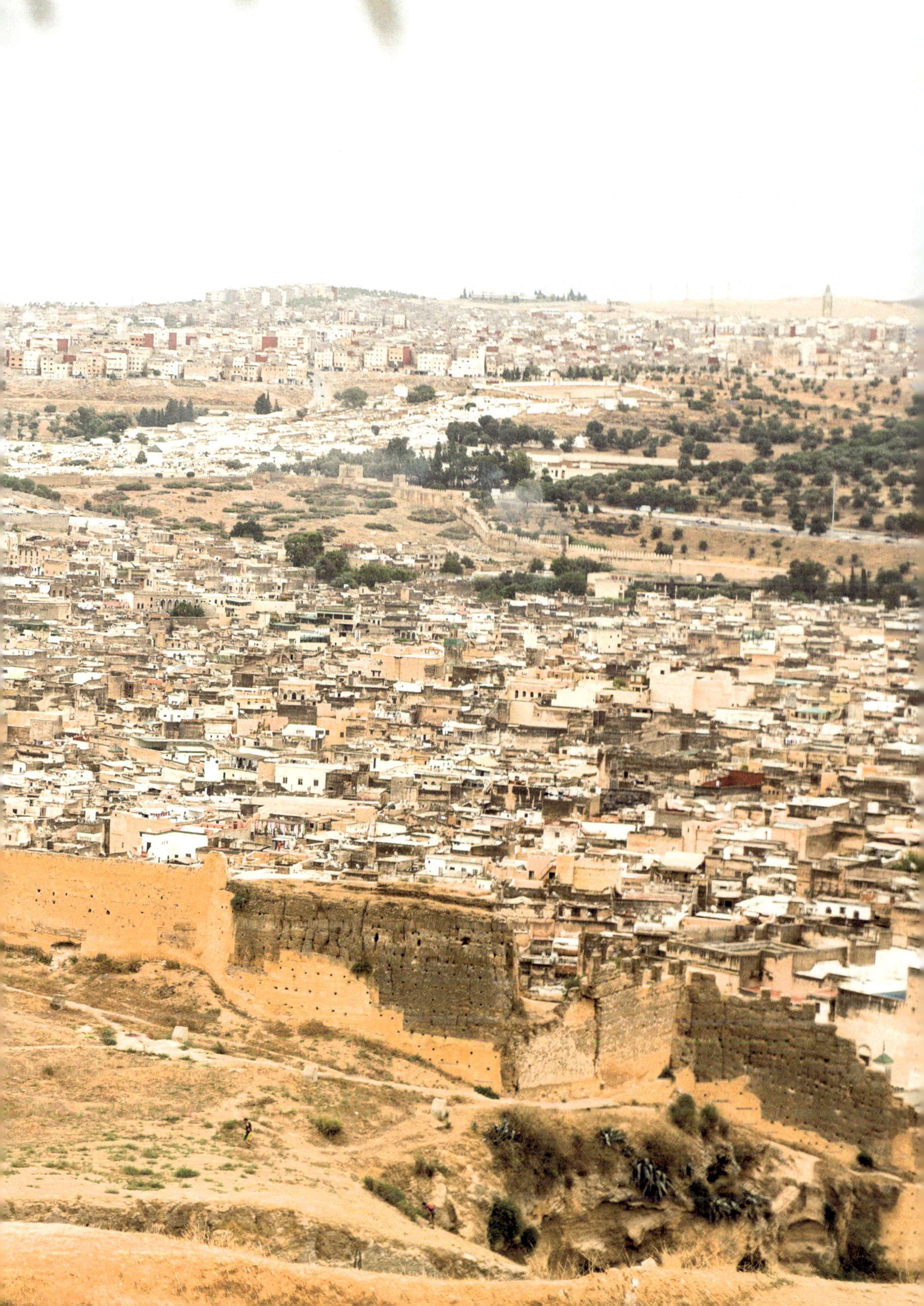

to non-Muslims. Our local fixer sneaked my recording devices into the mosque underneath his shirt, and with them he recorded the important Friday midday prayer, in the same room where the bell lamp is now hung.

There are five prayer calls each day, at which times one hears the most amazing multidirectional and multi-channel polyphony emitting from the numerous mosques in the Old Town (Medina) of Fez. I recorded each of the five prayer calls at a different spot in and near the Medina, from the rooftop of the now-abandoned Aben Danan Synagogue to the top of the ruins of the old city wall.

The sound-installation component of the work I am planning to make is taking shape in my head. It must involve some sort of multi-node timed operation, a sort of spatialized dissonance in unison. Just recently, Claire Bishop published an article in *e-flux* that discusses how artist-led-research leads often to a sort of inertia, an indifferent research-has-taken-place statement, but exerts no real opinions. I tend to agree. In his epistle, James makes the statement, "For as the body without the spirit is dead, so faith without works is dead also" (James 2:26). I think the reverse is also true: Works without faith—a devotion to a belief—are cynicism.

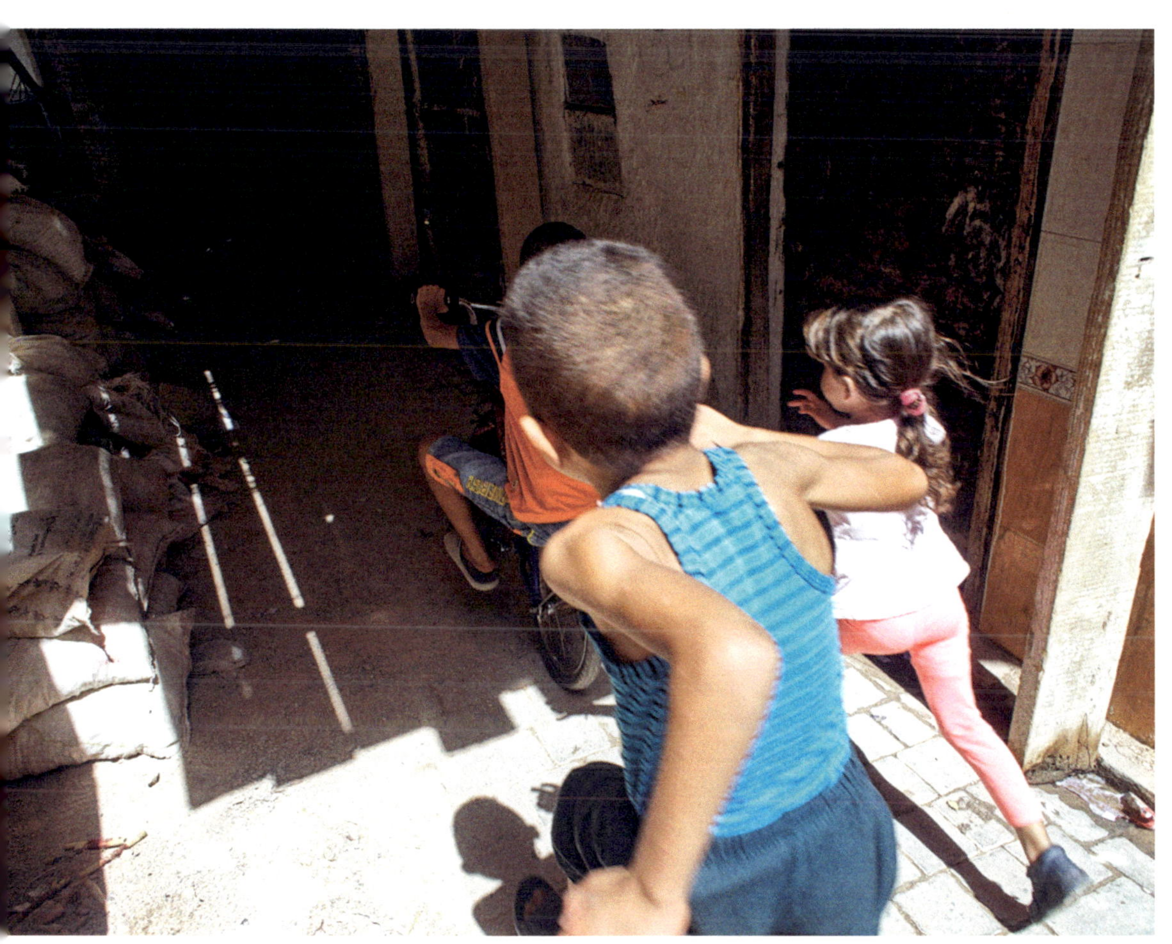

Morocco

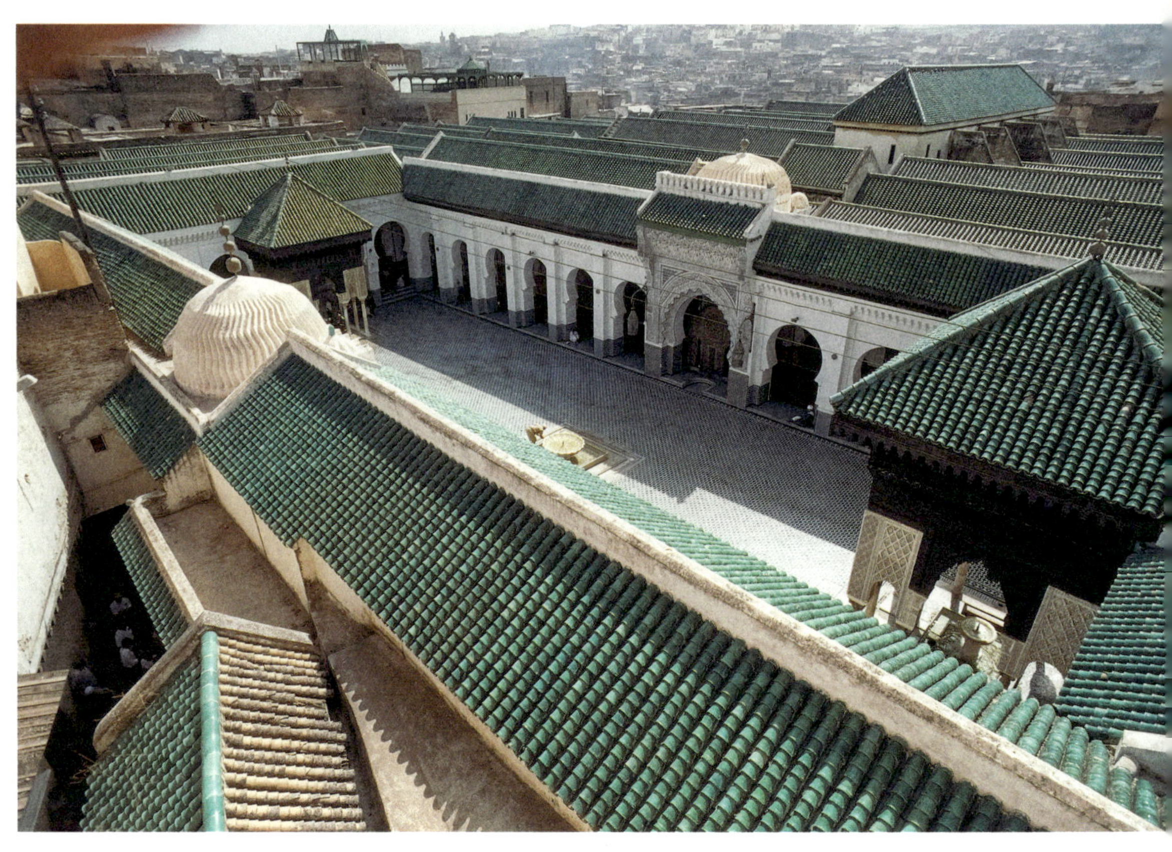

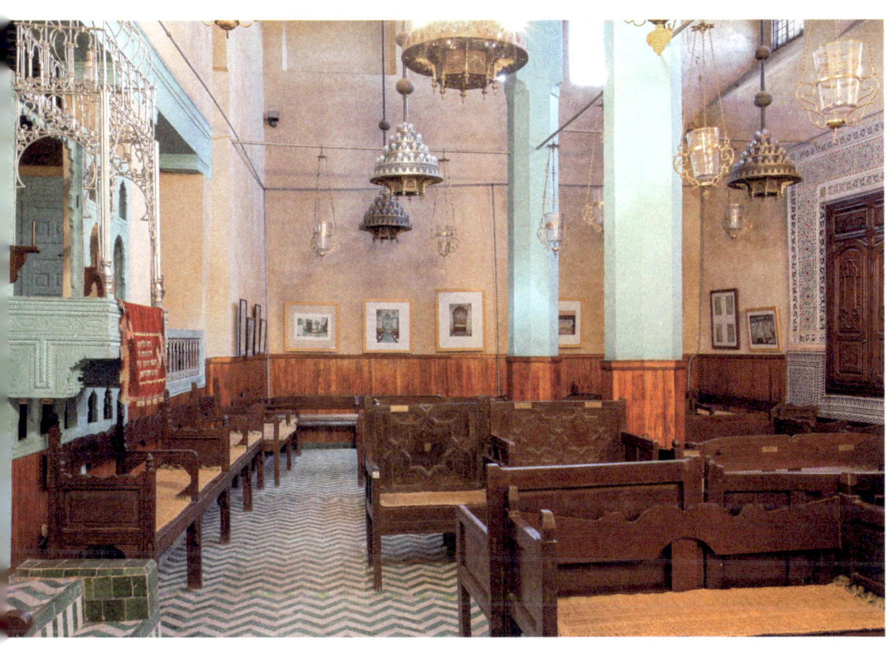

Kenya

Kenya was once a popular tourist destination and a peaceful nation where different beliefs coexisted in harmony. You see this in Mombasa's rich collection of Hindu temples, mosques, and churches of various denominations. These days, hardly a month goes by without news of exploding grenades, suspected homemade bombs, and kidnapping attempts. There is a real sense of insecurity wrought by indiscriminate terrorist acts.

The day of my arrival was marked by rumors of homemade bombs in a Nairobi shopping mall. My driver seemed on edge and exercised a high degree of caution throughout my stay. On my last day, I wanted to make a recording of the midday *adhan*, but to be seen with recording equipment near a mosque would have put both of us in danger of harassment. We found a parking spot opposite the mosque. With the vehicle's tinted windows rolled down, I placed the microphone on the backseat. The driver bought himself a plate of fruit from a nice boy across the street, so he could pretend that he had just parked to eat his lunch. The boy told us that the merciful call for prayers was due in thirty minutes. The rest of the meal passed in extremely tense silence.

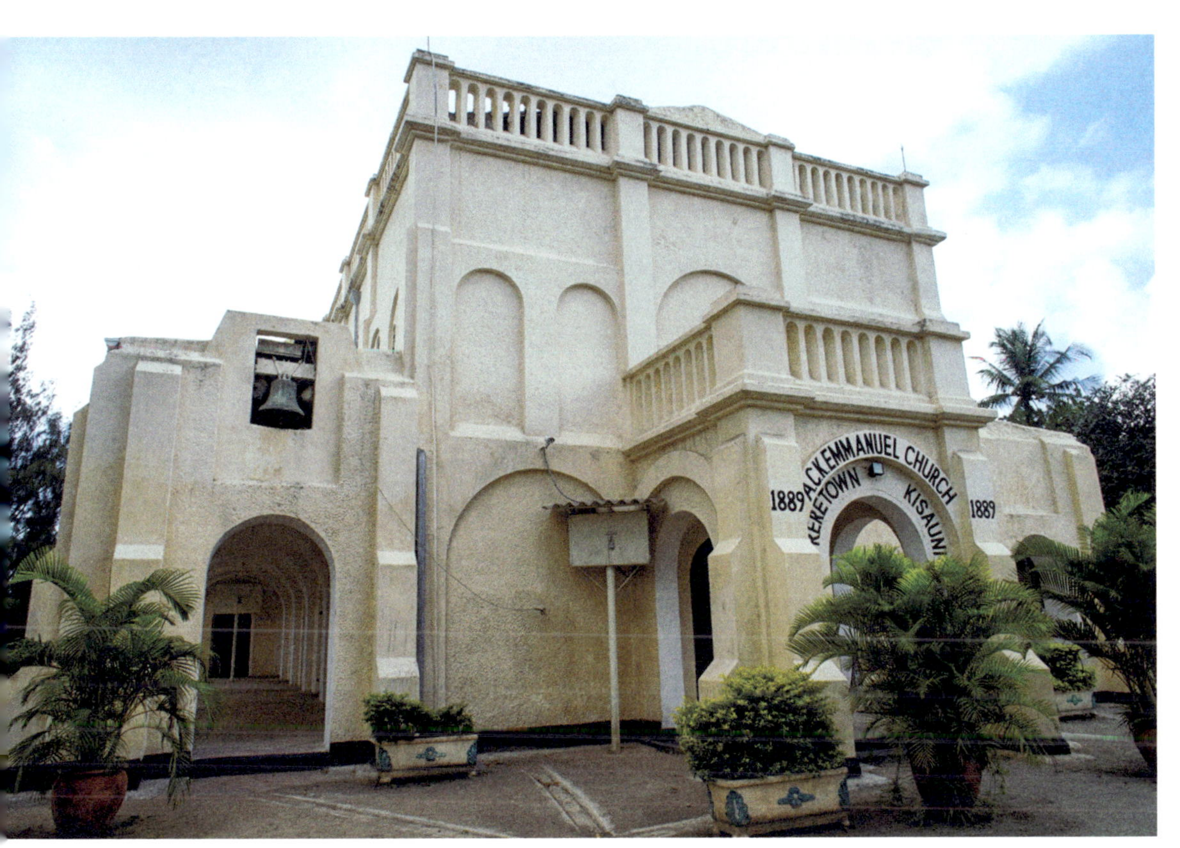AC KEMMANUEL CHURCH
1889
KERETOWN
KISAUNI
1889

I came to Mombasa to track down a "slave trader warning bell," but the current whereabouts of the bell and the circumstances surrounding its mysterious disappearance provide a glimpse into the nation's troubled history. The coastal city was once a major hub of the East African slave trade. A bell tower stands in the district of Kengeleni. Its bell was once used as an alarm to warn townsfolk of the approach of the Arabic slave traders. I was informed by the National Museums of Kenya that the bell had long been stolen. The institution created a vanity fiberglass bell in its place, fenced off the area, and declared the bell tower a national monument.

Upon arrival, I discovered that the bell tower is now empty —even the fiberglass cast is gone. I was referred by the museum to Mr. Habel, the head priest at the St. Emmanuel ACK Church, which is across the street from the Kengeleni bell tower. The vanity bell was cast out of the parish's bell, and the church was built by and for the freed slaves. Mr. Habel in turn connected me to Mr. David Mwambila, a retired clergyman, who told me a wildly different version of the story. According to him, the slave-warning bell had not been stolen, but was moved into the St. Emmanuel ACK Church for safekeeping—so that the bell that the church now uses for its services is in fact the original

Kengeleni bell. But this story doesn't match up with the inscriptions on the church bell, which indicate that it was cast in 1895. The Kengeleni bell tower must certainly have predated that?

The plot thickens: I visited Frere Town, where the freed slaves and their descendants have been resettled, and spoke with the village's chief. Apparently, in 2007 there was a court dispute in which the freed slaves' descendants attempted to take ownership of the St. Emmanuel ACK Church. As the rows intensified, the church's Sunday service was briefly suspended. The Frere Town village chief told me that the community has since dropped the case. He was not forthcoming about the reasons for the decision, but confirmed Mr. Mwambila's "relocation" story.

Exactly a month before my arrival, the United Kingdom finally lifted its travel warning to the coastal regions of Kenya. The town is still pretty much deserted. Here, owners of minivans display texts and graphics to distinguish themselves from other operators. I spotted one that said, "Tough times don't last." Another one read, "Thy grace is enough for me."

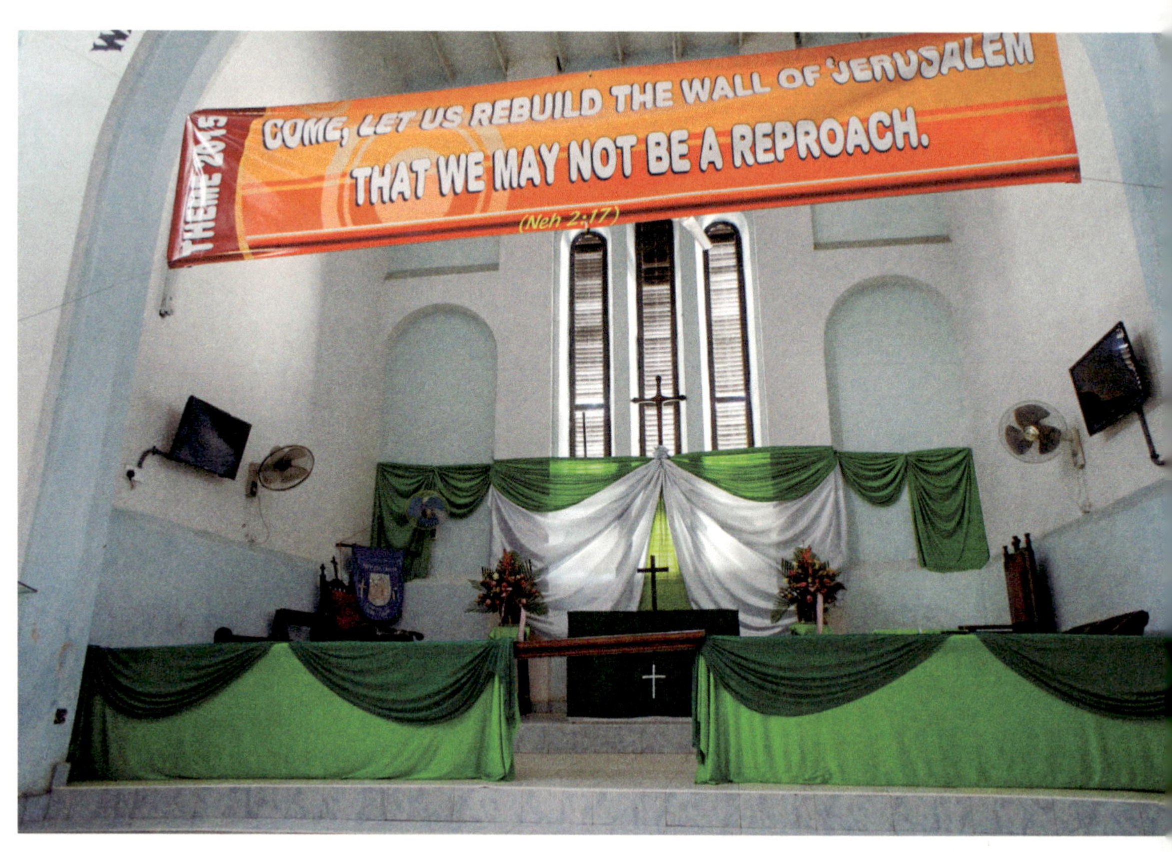

THEME 2015
COME, LET US REBUILD THE WALL OF JERUSALEM
THAT WE MAY NOT BE A REPROACH.
(Neh 2:17)

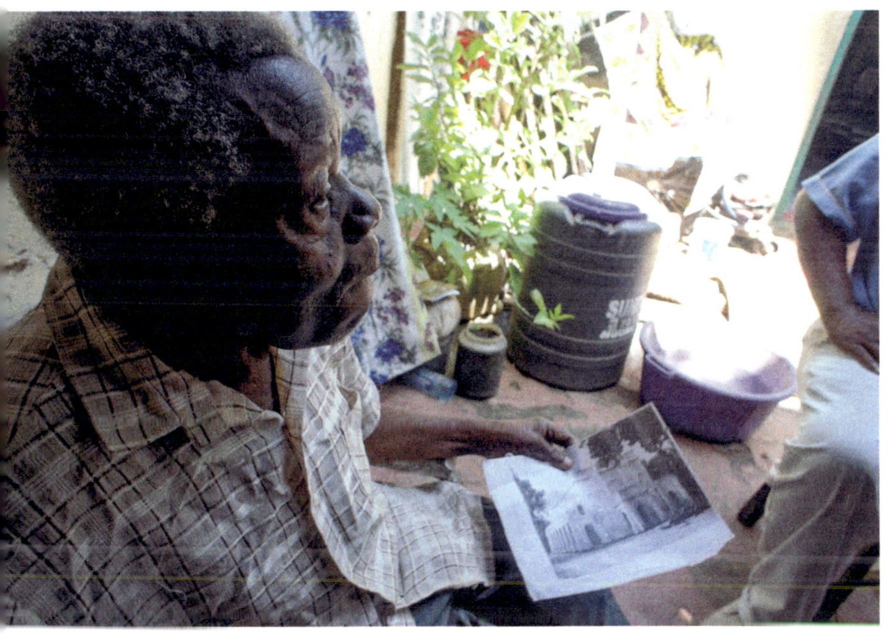

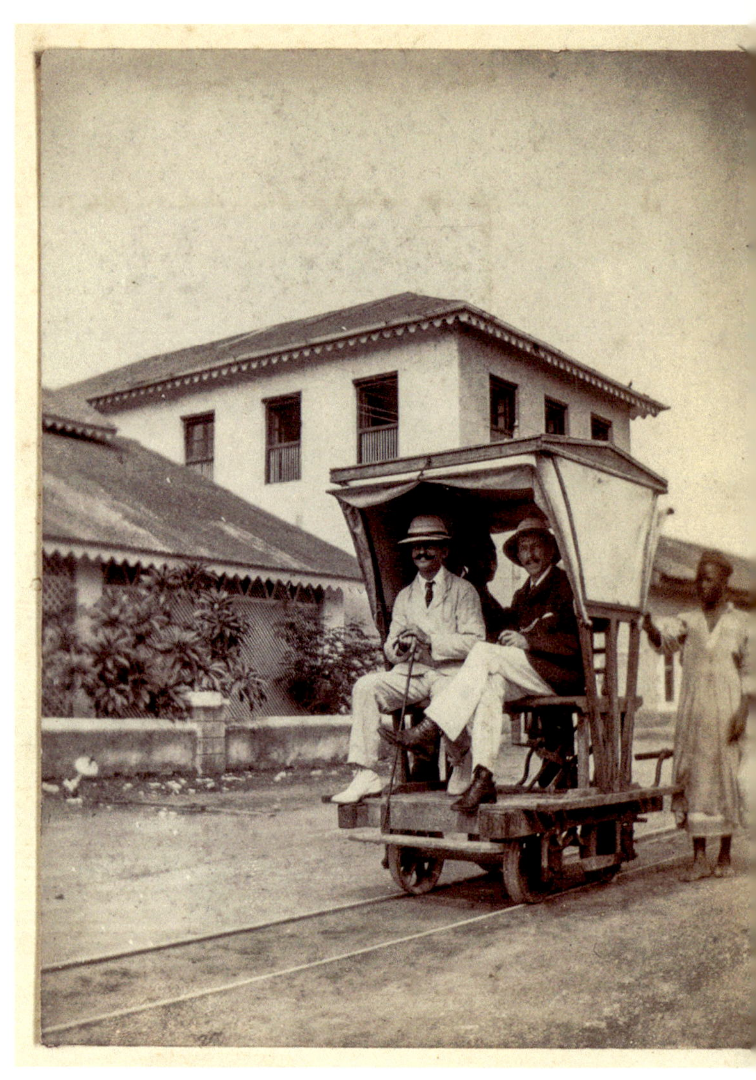

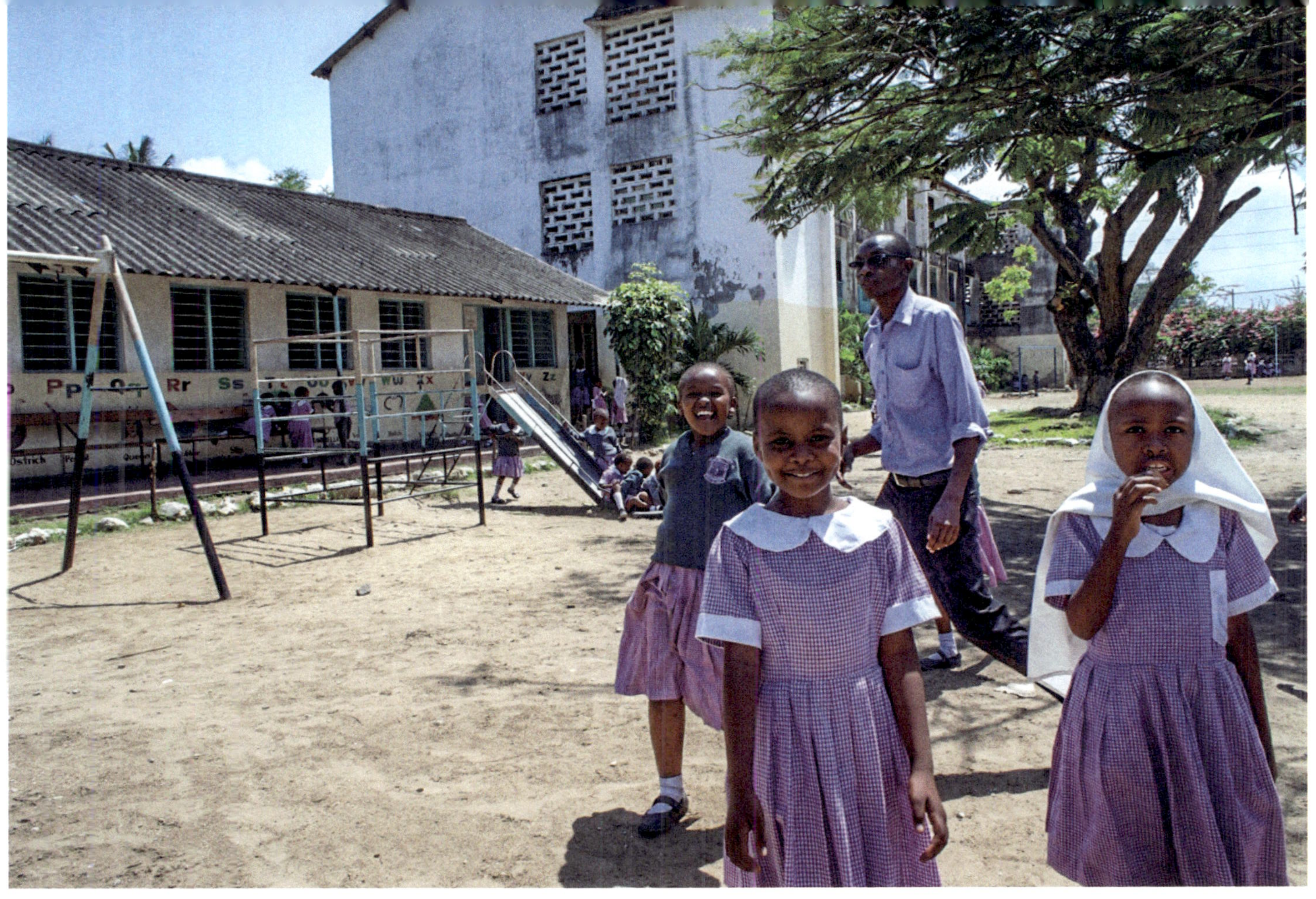

Kenya

Australia

I spent my puberty and formative years in the state of New South Wales, in Australia, at the height of far-right politician Pauline Hanson's power. I have many unpleasant tales of the lived interiority of ethnicity to tell, but I am determined to never bore you with them. I do not remember. My former assistant Marco used to say that when bad things happen, "it's character-building."

What I do remember with fondness is driving for long distances in the dark, past midnight, to unknown places, to meet unknown people. It was the age of IRC chat rooms, which facilitated many closeted teenagers' sexual enlightenment. When urges called, I'd wait until my parents were asleep, then sneak out to the family vehicle, map and torch in hand, and drive up to two hours to some random older boy's or man's house—mostly white, more often man than boy. In darkness every sound is amplified. Our garage roller-shutter made the most ridiculous noise. It is a sound that I have learned to associate with the feeling of guilt.

I landed in the airport of Melbourne on a Saturday evening. Five hours of nonstop driving later, I reached Darlington Point, in rural New South Wales, a community of one thousand inhabitants near the college town of

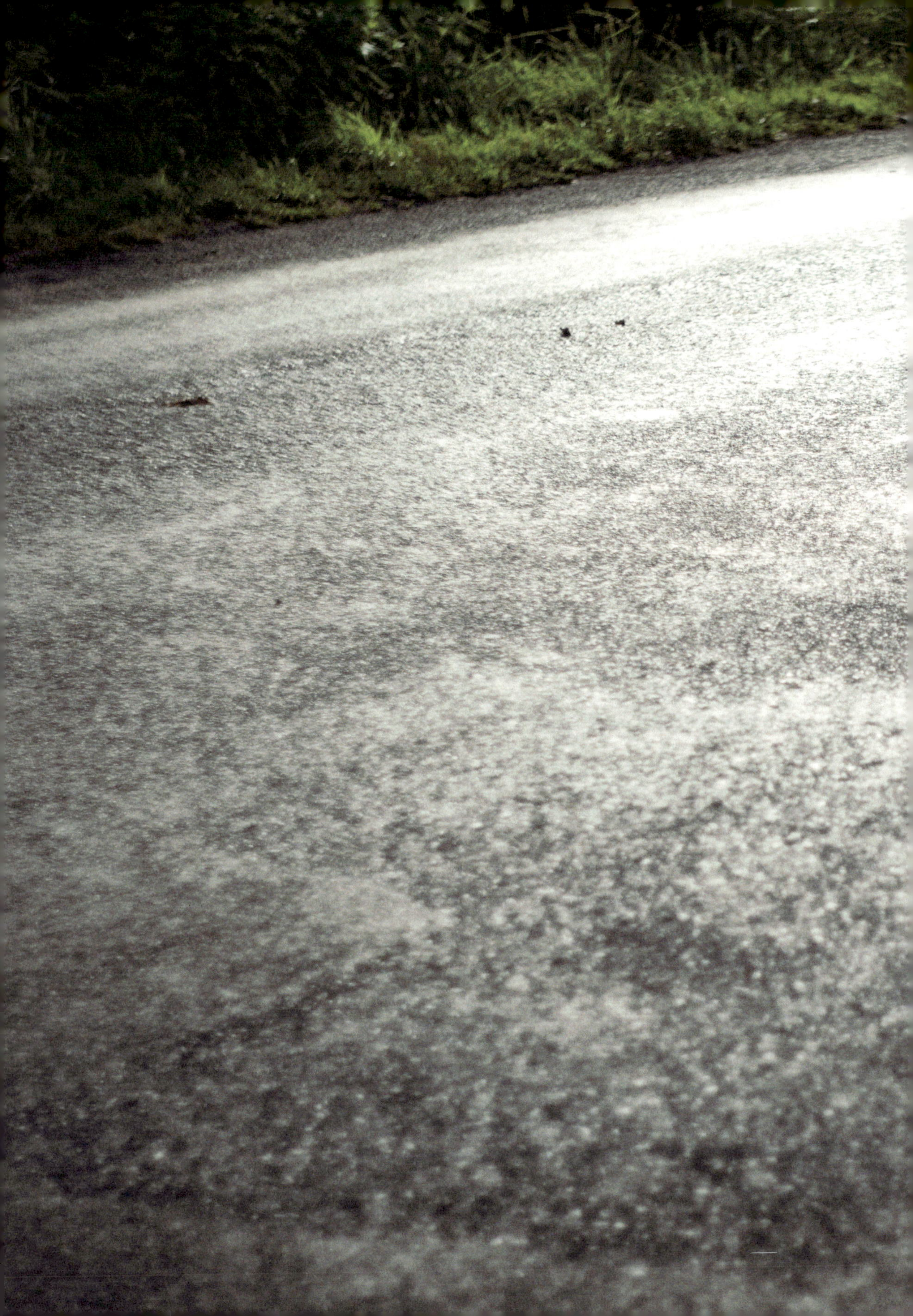

Griffith. My purpose was to visit the St. Paul's Anglican Church, which has in its possession a bell that came from the mission of English Rev. John Brown Gribble, also known as the Warangesda Mission.

The mission, established in 1880, provided services and education to the Aborigines of the area until it was disbanded in 1924. In the early twentieth century, black Australians were essentially barred from public education. School bells all over Australia rang only for white children. Some believed that the mission did good work for the people of Warangesda. But indigenous historian Philippa Scarlett, whom I connected with through her blog, contests these claims. In an email, she wrote, "Gribble's dairies recorded that he beat and imprisoned young women … and expulsion was a weapon used throughout the mission's history. Little boys were beaten." The quality of the education provided by the mission was uneven. As with the Kengeleni bell in Mombasa, there had also been attempts by some members of the Warangesda people to repossess the mission bell at St. Paul's.

I arrived at St. Paul's severely sleep-deprived. Shortly before 9 a.m. I was greeted by Mrs. Hutchins, who rang the bell for me and informed me that Rev. Sue Chilvers would not be joining us. I stepped inside the modest chapel. Five other members, including Mr. Hutchins, showed up for the morning prayer. I had never attended a service without a clergyman, but I was an Anglican schoolboy, so the proceedings were familiar to me. Afterward, Mrs. Hutchins showed me two beautiful volumes of a Bible that belonged to the mission. They spoke positively of Gribble. In the afternoon, I interviewed Heather Edwards, the daughter of an original member of the mission. She also spoke well of the mission, and dismissed the bell-repossession efforts as misguided. After the mission was disbanded, the children of the mission were relocated to mixed-race schools. Heather recounted that at her school, several white families demanded that special "no-blacks" toilets be constructed for their children.

This I do remember: I was the last to step inside of an elevator filled with other schoolchildren. A boy toward the back yelled, "No Asians in the elevator." Infuriated, I turned around, searched hard in my head for a counter-insult, but then said nothing. Had I answered back, the boy would have made my thick accent the new subject of his ridicule. So I worked hard on writing. Writing is not something that comes naturally to me. But it is easier to hide one's accent on paper.

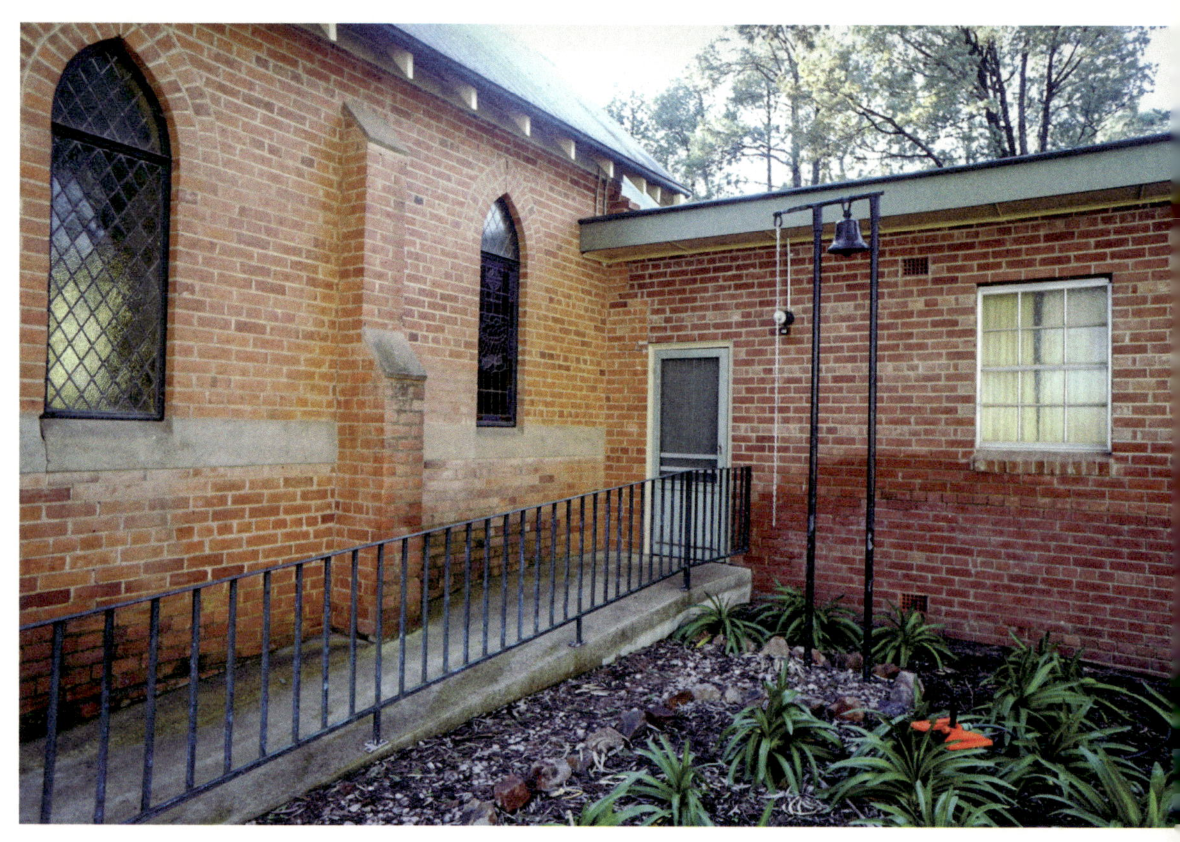

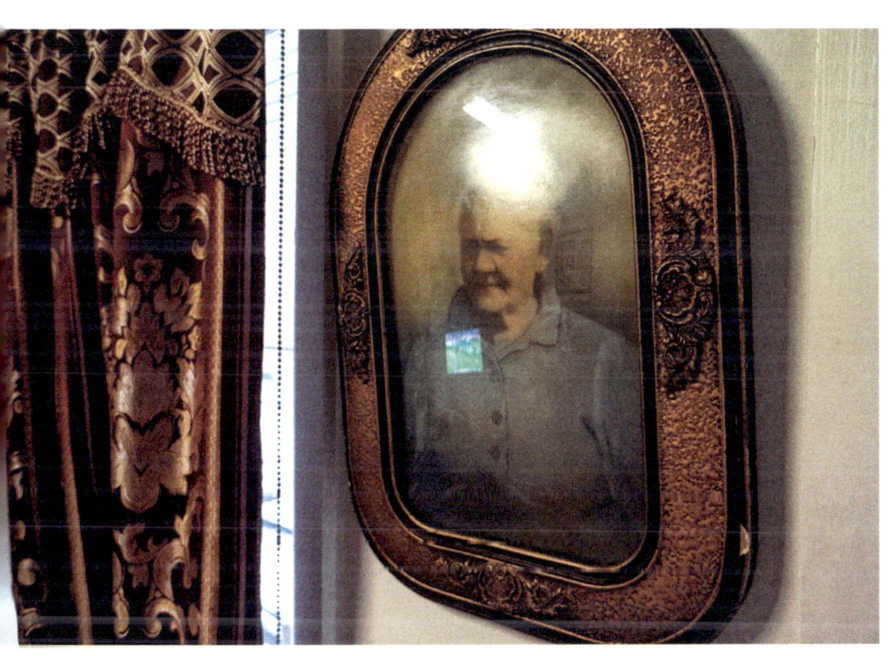

ANGLICAN CHURCH OF AUSTRALIA
Diocese of Riverina
Parish of Coleambally & Darlington Point
St.Pauls Church Darlington Point
HOLY EUCHARIST
MORNING PRAYER
1st Sunday 11am
3rd & 5th Sunday 9am
2nd & 4th Sunday 9am
PRIEST IN CHARGE:
Reverend Sue-Ellen Chilvers
Phone: 02 69544259 Mobile 0427 636 936
Email: anglicanparish.colydp@gmail.com

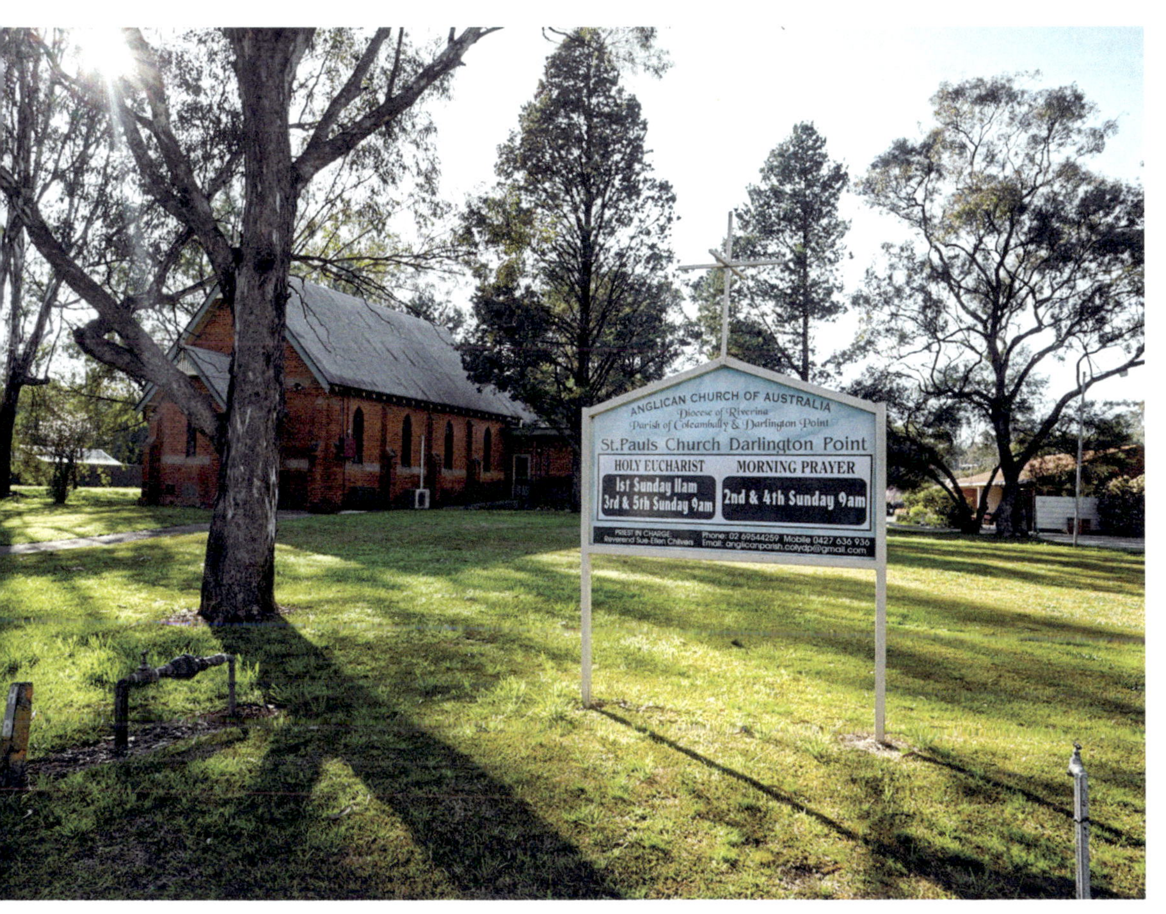

Australia

USA

Carillon at Tillman Hall at Clemson University, Clemson, USA
Korean Bell of Friendship, Angel's Gate Park, San Pedro, USA

Tillman Hall at Clemson University, in South Carolina, home to a beautiful carillon, was named after the ardent racist and lynch-law advocate "Pitchfork" Benjamin Tillman. Earlier this year, the name of the historic tower became the subject of a series of controversies, when some among the student population demanded that its name be changed. The discussion heated up considerably after the Charleston church shooting. I have some insight into the inner workings of a university. In situations such as this, the administration invariably defers responsibility to a task force. A task force is just what its name suggests: surplus energies of institutional logic. The process is object-oriented, outcome-focused, strategic, instrumental. (*Task force* as a terminology was first introduced by the U.S. Navy to describe improvised military maneuvers.)

Clemson was once a military college. The original Tillman bell signaled military changes throughout the day. It has since been moved across the street, and the new forty-seven-piece carillon is now heard at every quarter-hour. Professor Linda Dzuris, the university's first carillonneur, gave me a tour of the instrument. Carillons are performed by smashing one's bunched-up fist onto long wood pegs.

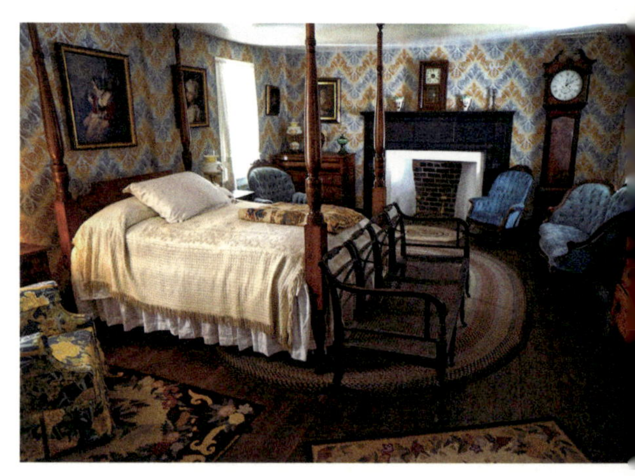

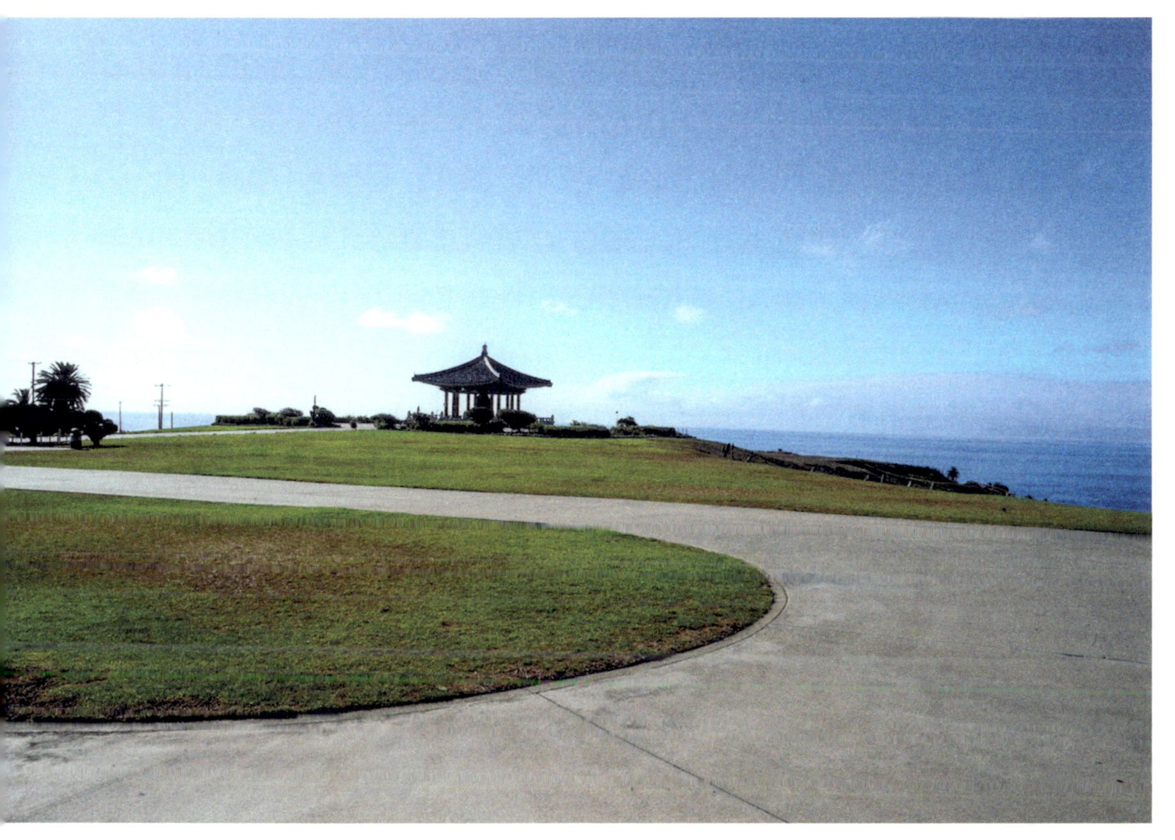

A single bell can weigh thousands of pounds, and there is no electrical assistance, so a considerable force is required to swing the instrument. Traditionally, the largest of the bells is tolled on the occasion of the death of a Clemson community member, with each sounding of the bell marking a year lived. The week prior to my visit, the bell tolled for a student who lived to twenty-three. Linda agreed to restage it for my recording. She played with a downward stroke that resembled the banging of the fist on a table—it befits the mourning of young, untimely death.

I was to make two stops in the United States. The first of the two stops was less successful: I intended to record the Korean Bell of Friendship at Angel's Gate Park, in San Pedro. This bell is supposed to ring on Constitution Day. Upon arrival, I was informed that the bell will not ring this year, for of the lack of a community partner. I spent a couple of days making sound sketches in the park instead. A small group of frustrated Korean tourists, who had learned the disappointing news upon arrival, vocalized the sound of the bell instead.

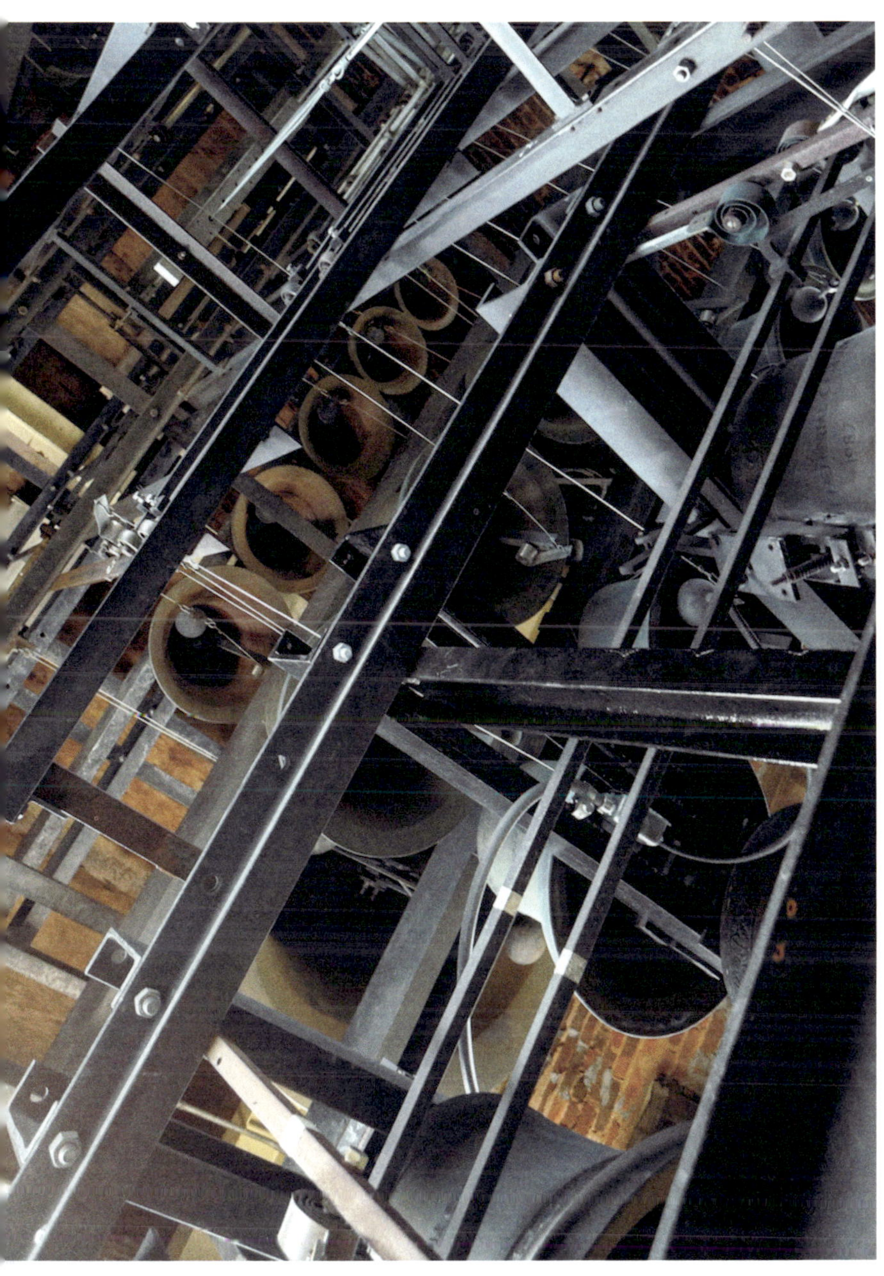

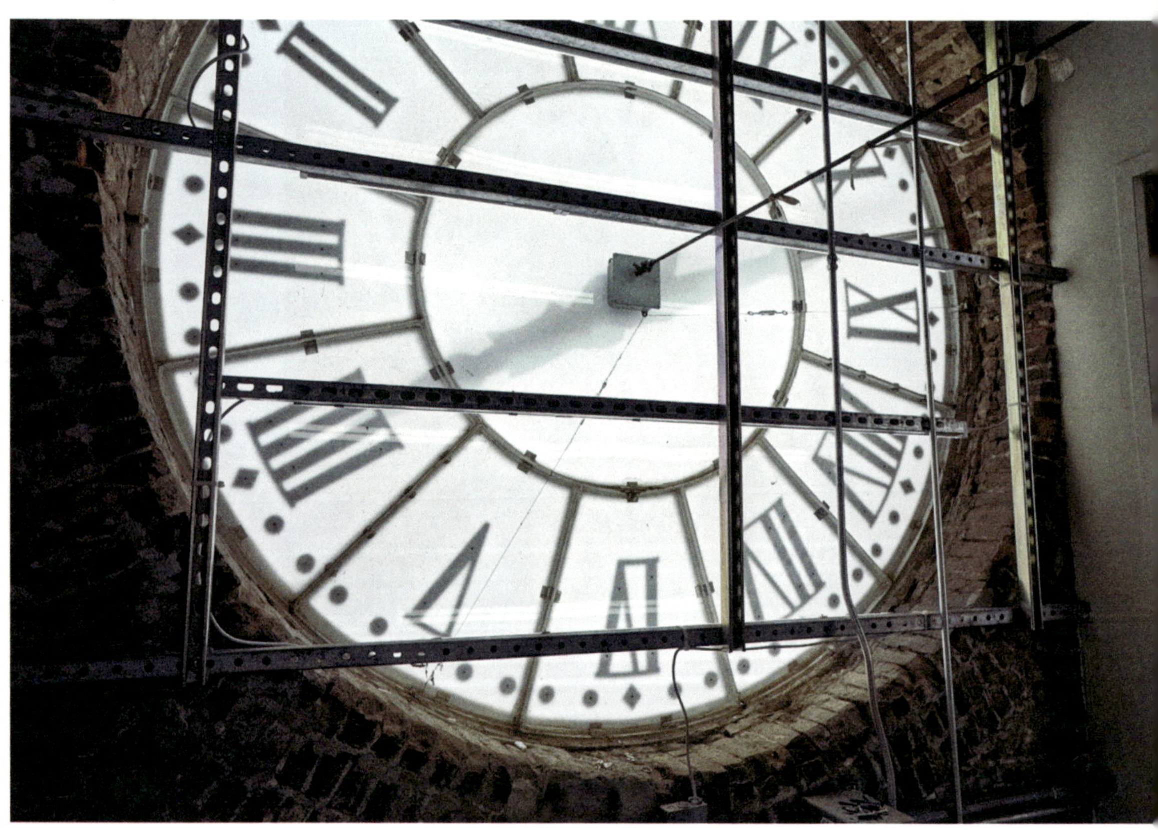

Austria

I came to Vienna for the Pummerin—the largest of the bells that adorn St. Stephen's Cathedral, widely known as the Stephansdom. Due to its fragility, the instrument is only tolled a few times a year. The original Pummerin was cast out of three hundred cannons that were left behind by the Turks during the Ottoman siege of Vienna. It was destroyed during World War II. In 1952, a new Pummerin was created out of the molten remains of the original bell and Turkish cannons from the Heeresgeschichtliches Museum.

I arrived at Stephansplatz early in the morning on National Day and settled in a corner with my art supplies. As at any celebratory occasion that calls for a public gathering in Europe these days, there was a general tenseness and a high degree of caution. The police came by to check on me several times. The smaller bells of Stephansdom sounded in a variety of combinations throughout the day. The real special moment came at 5 p.m., when the infrequently heard Pummerin first tolled on its own for fifteen minutes, and then provided a persistent ostinato to an urgent three-note pattern. The treble and the bass maintained rhythmic independence throughout, each occupying its own temporal space. While smaller bells speak with clarity and can be heard from afar, large bells are mostly felt. They produce waves of deep, voluminous vibration that engulf

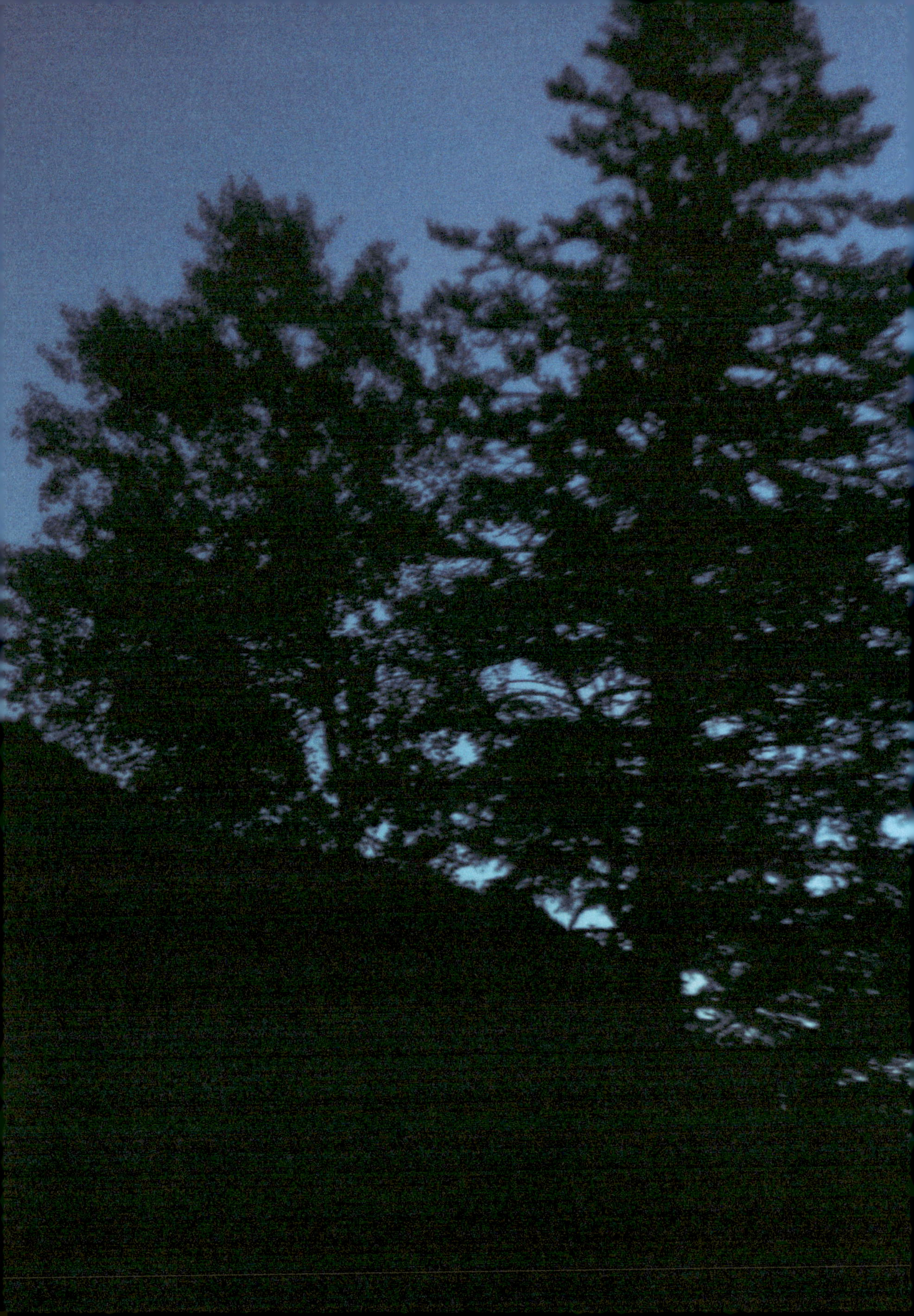

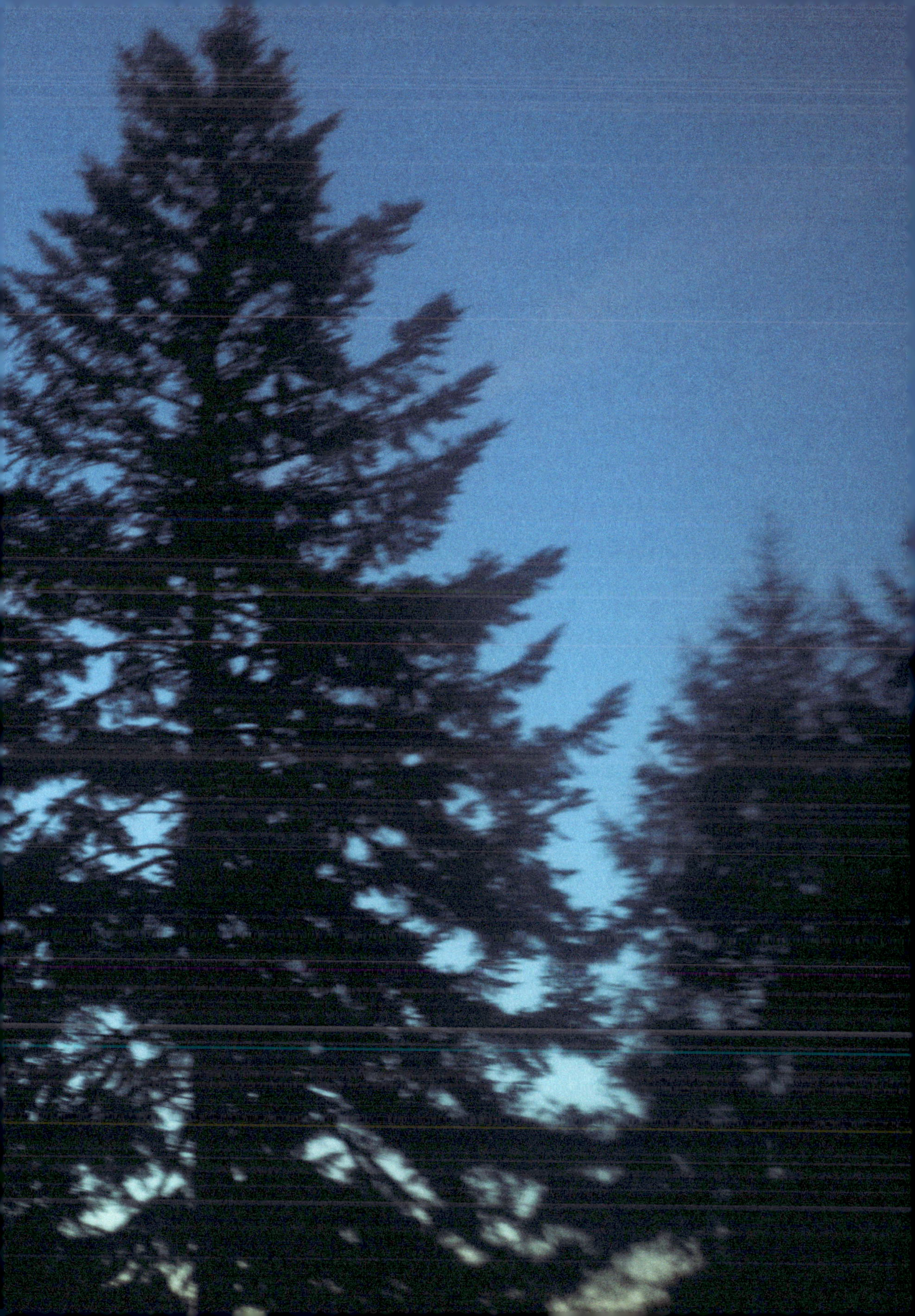

and ground the soul. *How could anybody not find the Pummerin's sound beautiful?* I thought to myself. The profundity of experiences such as these exposes moral relativism as a lie. But then I am reminded of several court cases that I came across in my research, in which residents living near bell towers attempted to put a stop to the regular tolling. There could be too much of a beautiful thing. Sound, even a beautiful one, has moments of aggression, and it does not care to be contained. Ideologies behave in the same manner. The operative logic of moral courage is the extension of invitations, not impositions. The next morning, we arrived at Innsbruck. The Pummerin's maintenance service is provided by the Grassmayr bell foundry in this sleepy resort town. In the afternoon, I recorded the bells of a nearby monastery, which are also the proud creations of the Grassmayr. A day later, we left for the "peace bell" in South Tyrol, which tolls daily at 5 p.m. The bell is located in a remote hilltop. At 4:55 p.m., a technician came to start the bell. We were its lone pilgrims in this bitterly cold afternoon. But the bell couldn't care less.

Throughout history, the bell has called us to take arms, to pray, to gather, to flee, to celebrate, and to mourn—but it has absolutely no opinion about us. The sensorial pleasure that it affords is disinterested. It draws the world in but also keeps it at arm's length. For all and for nobody it tolls.

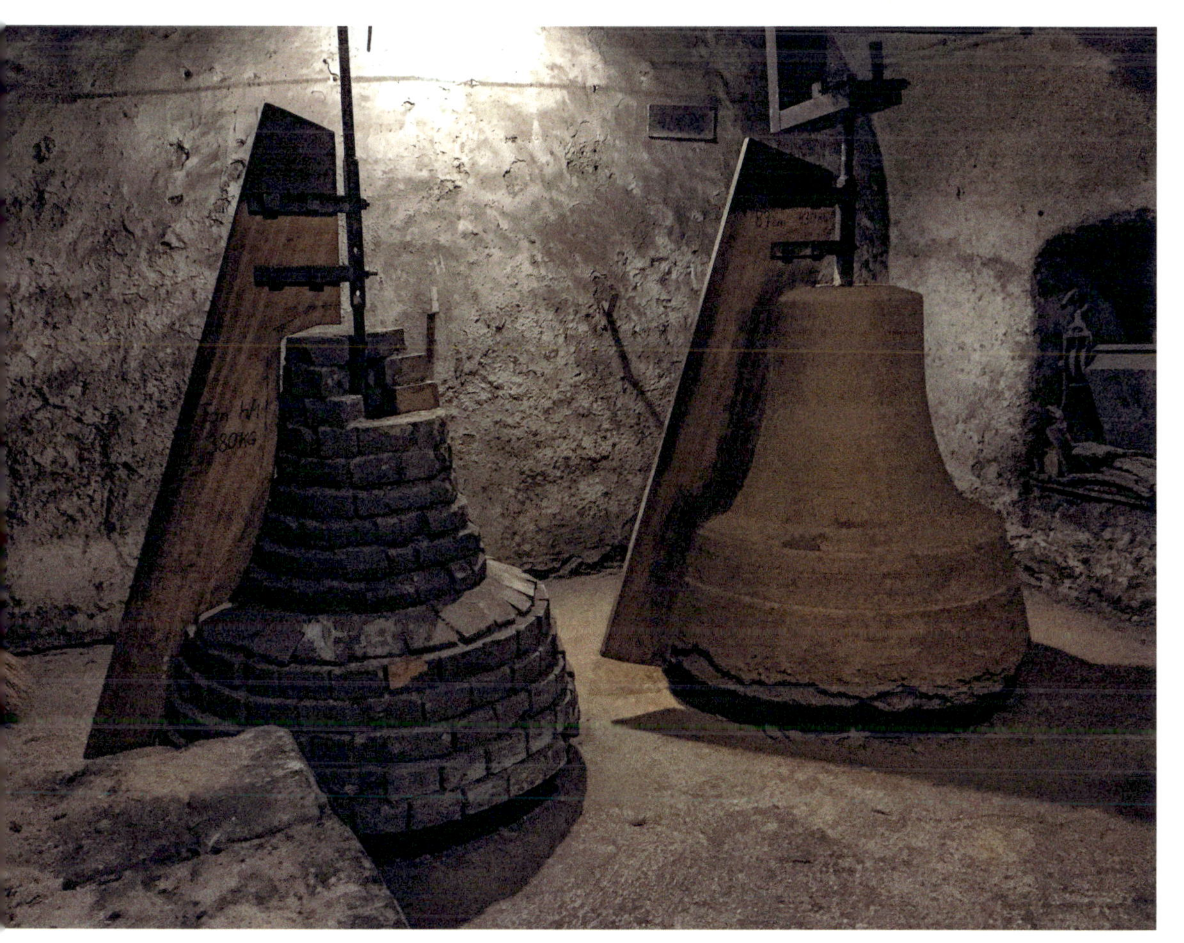

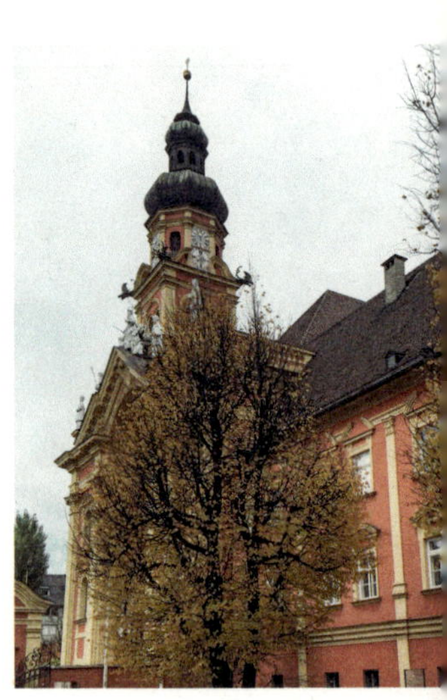

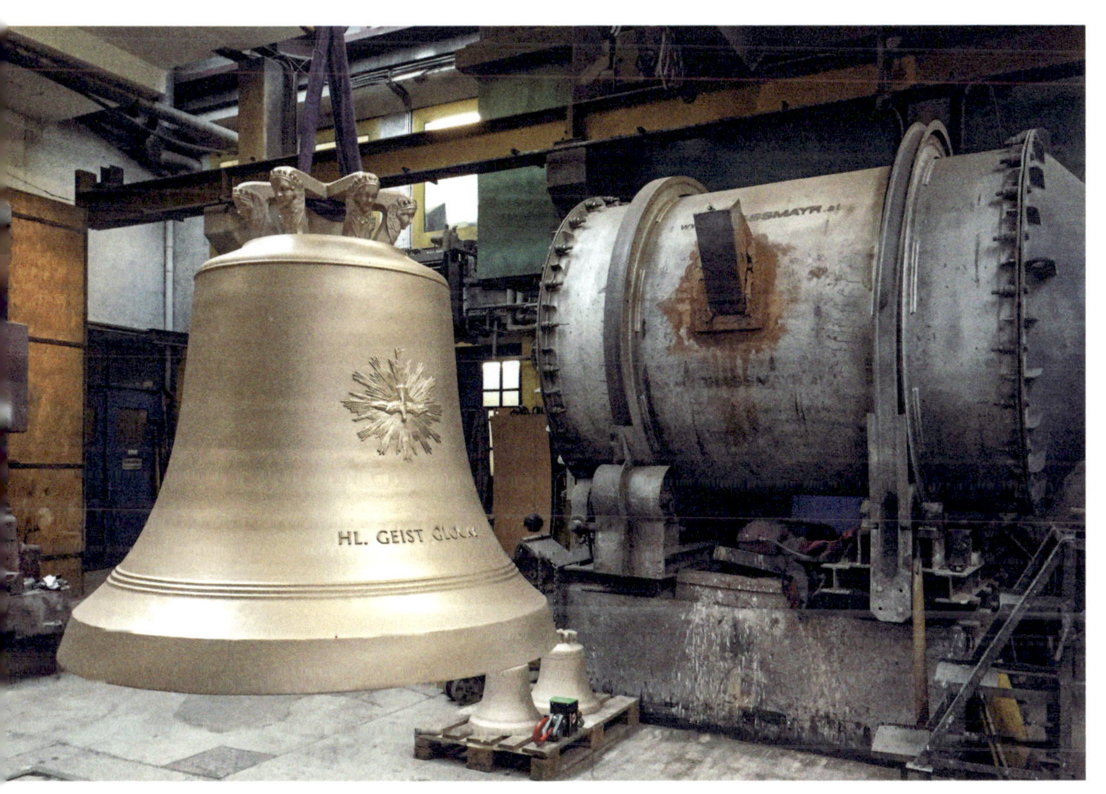

Austria

So You Are Old
by the Time
You Reach the Island

So You Are Old by the Time You Reach the Island is
a "multimedia walk" with site-specific video, radio
broadcast, and live-performance elements.
Each participant was given a "kit" that contained
an iPod, a map, a booklet, and various small objects.
The sixty-minute-long journey outlined a fictitious
world of sonic warfare between nations, unfolding
along the coastline of Admiralty, in Hong Kong.

Synopsis

The Ministry of Gentlemanly Warfare (MGW) is an
underground organization (of unidentified national
origin) that conducts forms of "sonic sabotage."
The organization conceals its existence for security
purposes and operates behind various fictitious
branches of the Naval Force (in official records, it is
often referred to as the "Joint Technical Board").

One of its most important duties has been the installation of limited-range clandestine radio broadcasts,
which can be picked up on hijacked FM frequencies
at specific locations of a city. As with most clandestine radio operators, the ministry's aim is to sway
political opinion through sound. What distinguishes
its broadcast, however, is the fact that its signals
are not transmitted to the populace at large, but
can only be picked up within small targeted areas.

The effect is this: Seemingly out of nowhere, songs
of protest or revolutionary slogans exert themselves
on unassuming listeners as they drive, walk, or wander

through the city. Only moments later, the poetry of sonic propaganda cross-fades into commercial broadcast. Listeners wonder if they are in a lucid dream as their bodies move in and out of zones of ideological ether. The ministry altogether prefers this method of broadcasting, and transmission zones are referred to endearingly as "islands" in the organization's internal communications.

Premise

The audience follows Zhi-Lok (Lok), a senior engineering officer at the Radio Unit of the Ministry of Gentlemanly Warfare, as he installs the test signals for site-specific clandestine broadcasts along the waterfront of Admiralty on the ministry's directive.

Those who are interested in the mysterious work of the ministry and its history are known as "researchers." With a notebook, a media player (iPod Touch), a map, and various small objects, which were passed down to the audience by a researcher of unknown intention and origin, the audience sets out on a journey to recover Lok's radio test signals. Various media contents are available on the device, from Lok's monologues to photographs documenting his travel to film clips produced by the unknown researcher. The film modulates between a documentary-style film depicting Lok's classified operation and a dramatic monologue that reveals the mental processes of the protagonist.

At various locations, the audience is instructed to tune to specific FM frequencies for the test signals that Lok has left behind. Active researchers working in the field are distinguished by the possession of a toy trumpet—which is the main symbol in the official badge of the Radio Unit of the Ministry of Gentlemanly Warfare.

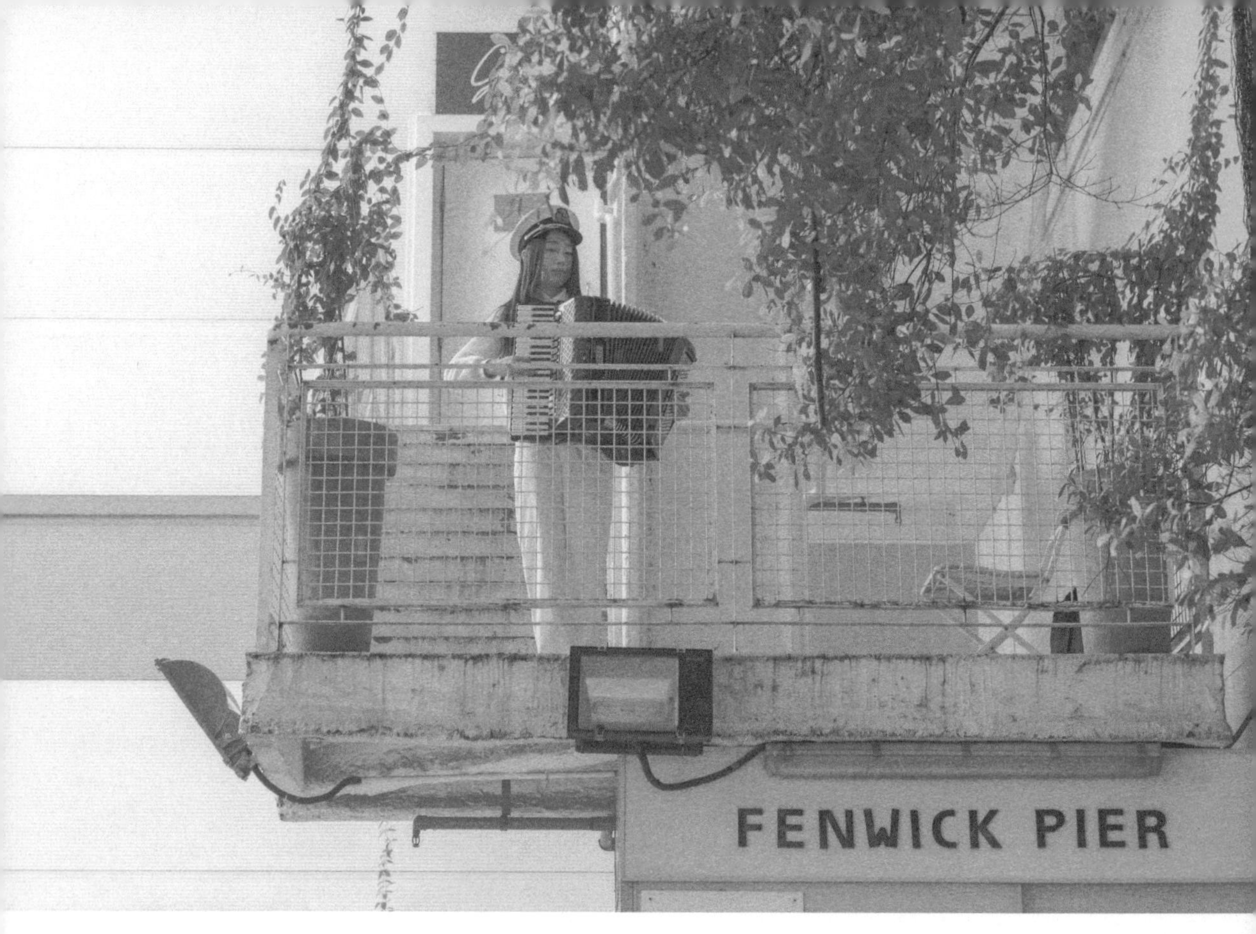

FENWICK PIER

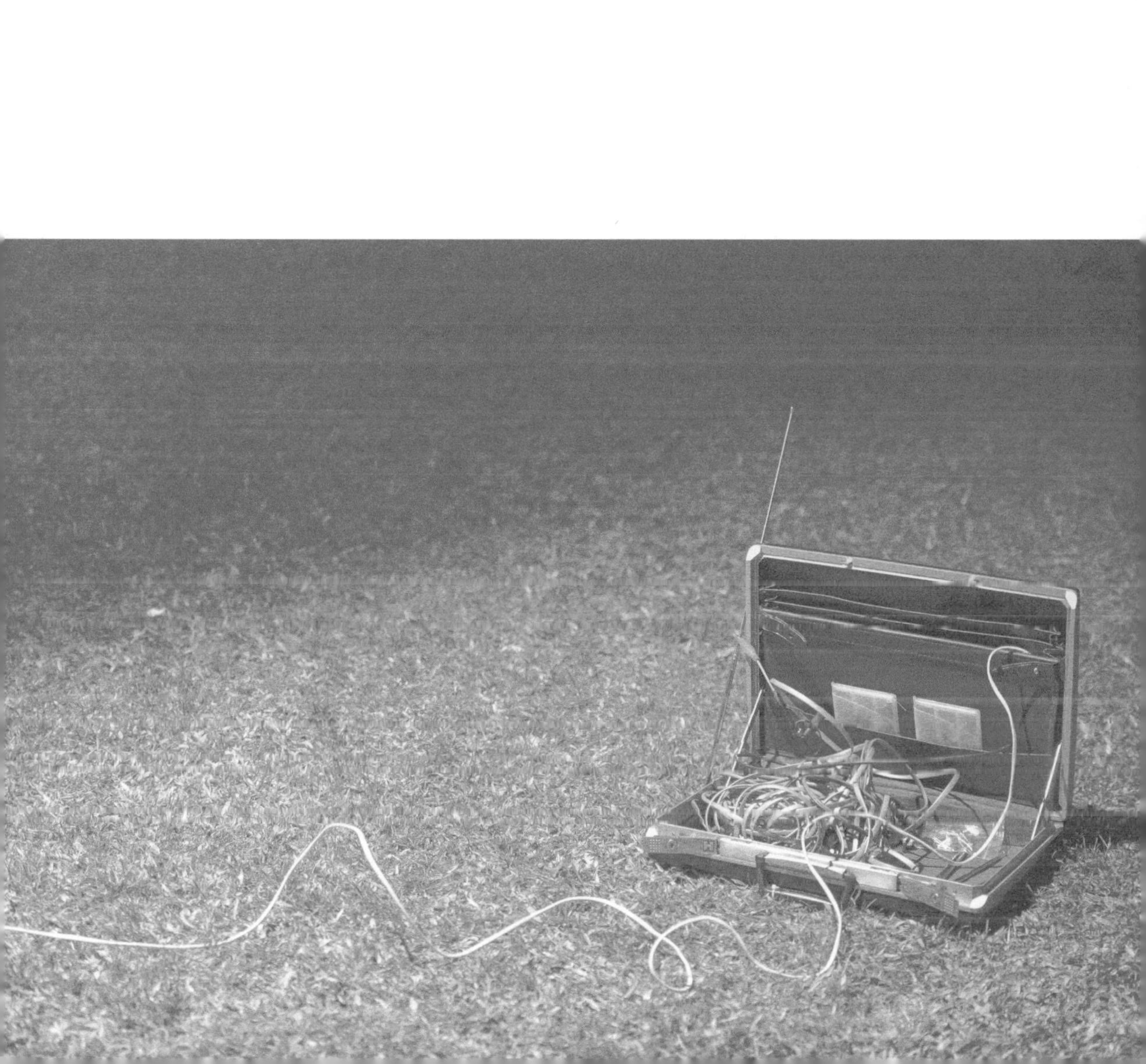

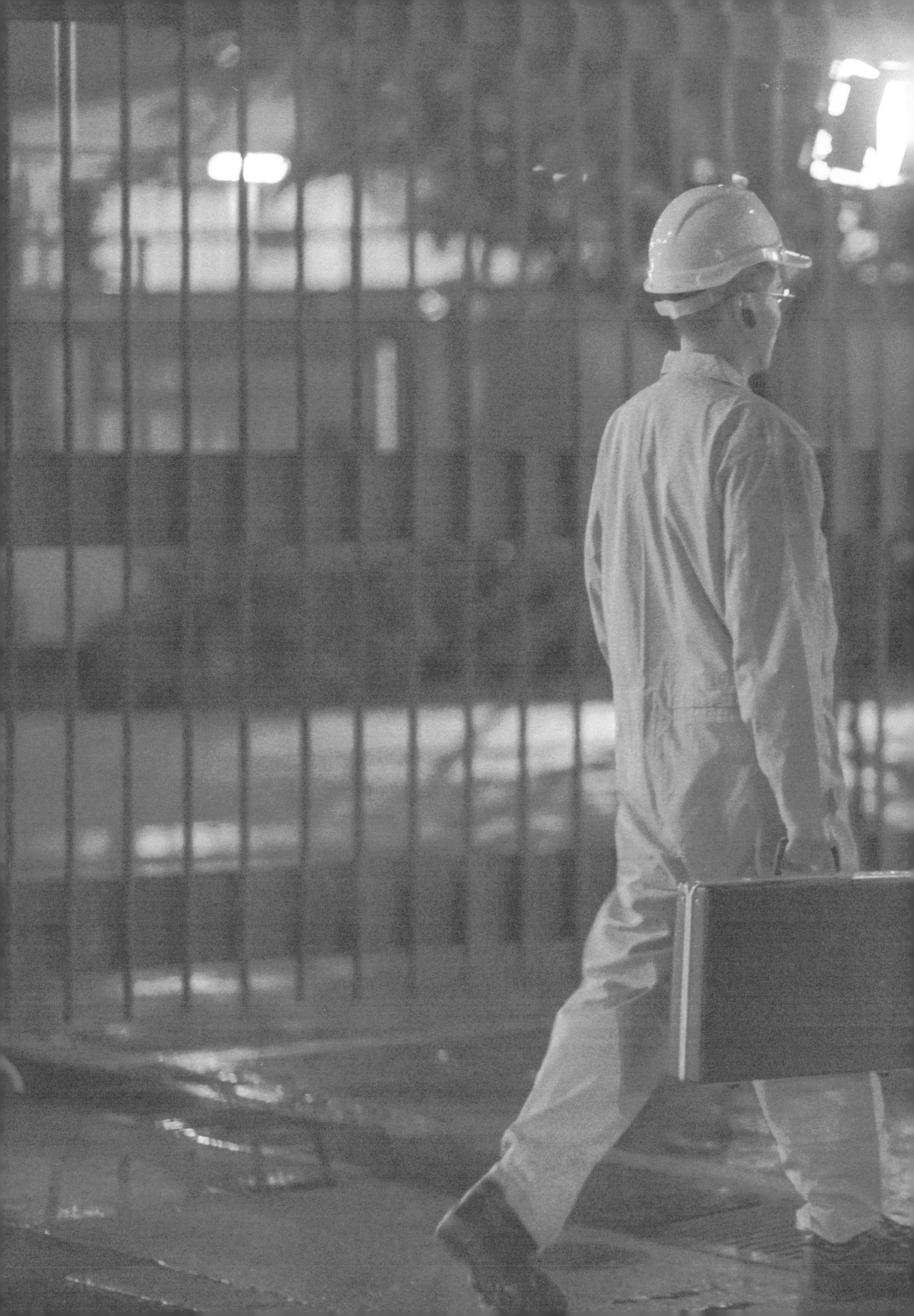

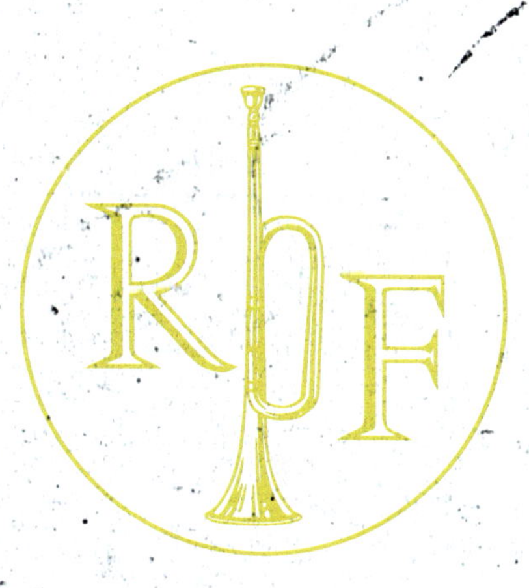

SO YOU
ARE OLD
BY THE
TIME YOU
REACH THE
ISLAND

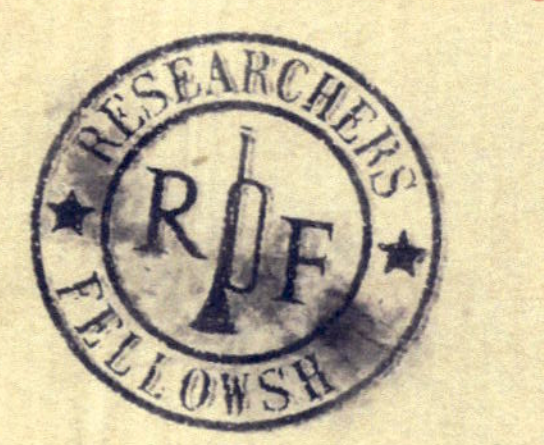

RESEARCHERS
FELLOWSHIP

Je K

009P/C122252

From: Researcher 0993

To: New recruits

Subj: Ministry of Gentlemanly Warfare

Encl: Map of test signal locations
(operation: Admiralty)

1. Ministry of Gentlemanly Warfare (MGW): an underground
organisation (of unidentified national origin) that conducts forms of
"sonic sabotage." The organisation conceals its existence for security
purposes and operates behind various fictitious branches of the
Naval Force (in official records, it is often referred to as the
"Joint Technical Board").

2. One of the ministry's most important work has been the
installation of limited-range clandestine radio broadcasts, which
can be picked up on hijacked FM frequencies at specific locations of a
city. As with most clandestine radio operators, the ministry's aim is
to sway political opinion through sound. What distinguishes their
broadcast however is the fact its signals are not transmitted to the
populace at large, but can only be picked up within small targeted
areas.

3. The effect is this: seemingly out of nowhere, songs of
protest or revolutionary slogans exert themselves on the unassuming
listener as they drive, walk, or wander through the city. Only
moments later, the poetry of sonic propaganda cross-fades into
commercial broadcast. Listeners wonder if they were in a lucid dream
as their bodies move in and out of zones of ideological ether.

4. The ministry altogether prefer this method of broadcast, and
transmission zones are referred to endearingly as "islands" in the
organisation's internal communications.

Researcher 0993

By direction

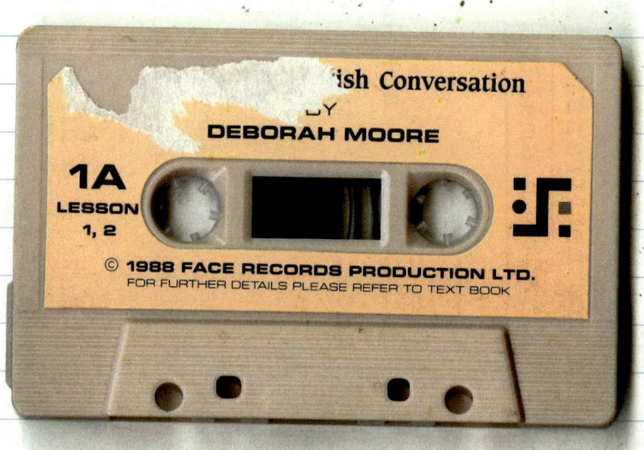
lish Conversation
BY
DEBORAH MOORE
1A
LESSON
1, 2
© 1988 FACE RECORDS PRODUCTION LTD.
FOR FURTHER DETAILS PLEASE REFER TO TEXT BOOK

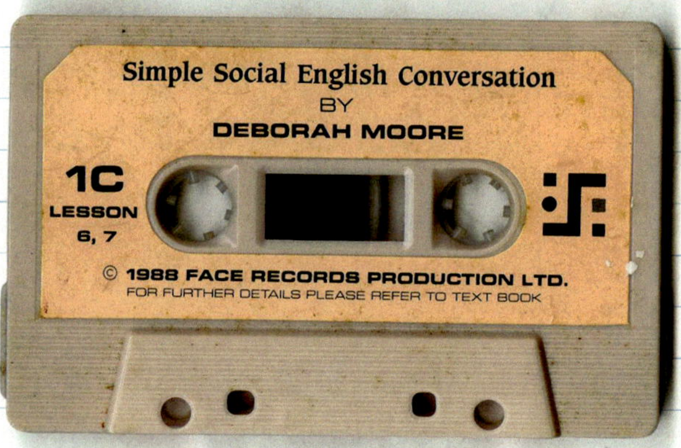
Simple Social English Conversation
BY
DEBORAH MOORE
1C
LESSON
6, 7
© 1988 FACE RECORDS PRODUCTION LTD.
FOR FURTHER DETAILS PLEASE REFER TO TEXT BOOK

LESSON FIVE 第五課

ASKING DIRECTIONS 問路

CONVERSATION : A – Tourist 遊客
B – Passer-by 過路人

A : Excuse me. Can you help me I think I'm lost.
對不起，您可以幫我嗎？我想我是迷路了。

B : Certainly. Where would you like to go?
當然可以，您想到那兒去呢？

A : Can you tell me where the Pearl Hotel is?
您可以告訴我明珠酒店在那兒呢？

B : Just keep going along the main road. You can't miss it.
只要沿著大路走，您不會看不見的。

A : Thank you very much.
非常感謝您。

B : Not at all. Are you new in town?
那裏話，您剛來這兒嗎？

A : Yes, I'm a stranger here. [Tourist, Visitor]
是的，在這兒我是人生路不熟。〔遊客，訪客〕

USEFUL PHRASES AND VOCABULARY

Can you help me?
您可以幫我忙嗎？

I think I'm lost.
我想我是迷路了。

Can you show me the way?
您可以告訴我該怎麼走嗎？

Where are we now?
我們現在身在何方？

Where am I now?
我現在身在何方？

Can you tell me how to get to....[destination]?
您可以告訴我怎樣到……〔目的地〕去嗎？

How far is it from here?
從這走有多遠呢？

Is it within walking distance?
是否離這不遠呢？

How far is it to walk?
要走多遠呢？

Can I walk there in....[minutes]?
我可以走……〔幾分鐘〕就到了嗎？

Where is the ....[destination]?
〔目的地〕……在那兒呢？

Is this.......[destination]?
這裏是……〔目的地〕嗎？

I am lost.
我迷路了。

Where would you like to go?
你想到那兒去呢？

Turn left 往左拐/向左轉	Turn right 往右拐/向右轉
Go up 往上走	Go down 往下去

LESSON THREE 第三課

AT A HOTEL 在酒店

CONVERSATION: A – Receptionist 接待員
B – Guest 客人

A : Good afternoon, Sir. May I help you?
午安，先生，有什麼我可以效勞嗎？

B : I would like to check in, please?
我想辦理入住手續

A : Do you have a reservation?
您有沒有預訂房間呢？

B : My travel agent has made reservations for me.
我的旅行社已經爲我預訂了。

A : May I have your name, please?
請問您的名字是……？

B : My name is John Smith.
我的名字是約翰史密夫。

A : Yes. sir, You have reserved a single room. Will you fill in this form, please?
對了，先生，您預訂了一個單人房間。請您填一填這張表格吧。

B : Certainly. Can you help me fill in this form?
好的，你可以幫我填這張表嗎？

A : Just write down your name, address and passport number.
寫上您的姓名、地址和護照號碼就行了。

B : Can I have a room with a view?
我可以要一個窗外有遠景的房間嗎？

A : Certainly, sir. Here is your key. Room number 123.
當然可以，先生，這是您（房間）的 鑰匙，是第 123 號房間。

B : Can you send someone to help me with my luggage?
你可以找人替我拿行李嗎？

A : The porter will help you. Enjoy your stay!
服務員會幫您的，希望您在這兒居停愉快！

USEFUL PHRASES AND VOCABULARY

I would like to change my reservation. [room]
我想更改一下我預定的房間。

I would like to deposit my valuables in your safe. [I would like to open a safety deposit box.]
我想把我的貴重物品存放在你的保險庫裏。〔我想開一個保險箱。〕

Could you please give me a morning call at seven tomorrow?
你可以明兒早上七點給我一個電話叫我起來嗎？

What is the rate for a single/double room per night?
單人/雙人房間每個晚上（每天）收費多少？

What time is check-out time?
什麼時候要辦退房手續？

Is there a laundry service in this hotel?
酒店有沒有洗衣服務呢？

Is there an airport bus from this hotel?
有公共車從這酒店往機場嗎？

Where is the nearest shopping centre? [bank, restaurant]
最近的購物中心在那兒呢？〔銀行，酒樓/餐廳〕

Room Service	客房服務	Lobby	大堂（酒店大堂）
Porter	服務員	Maid (Bell Boy)	女待（門僮）

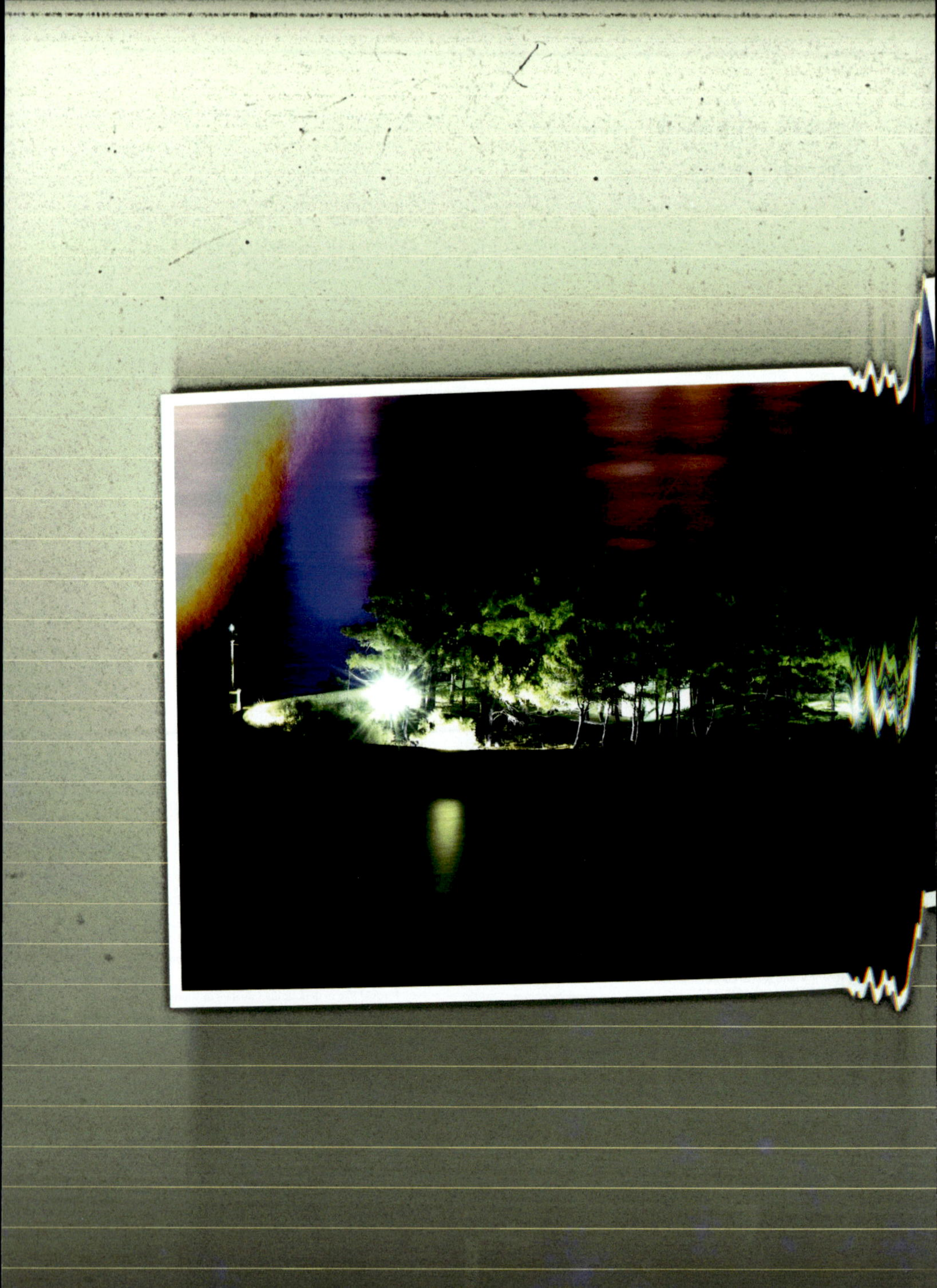

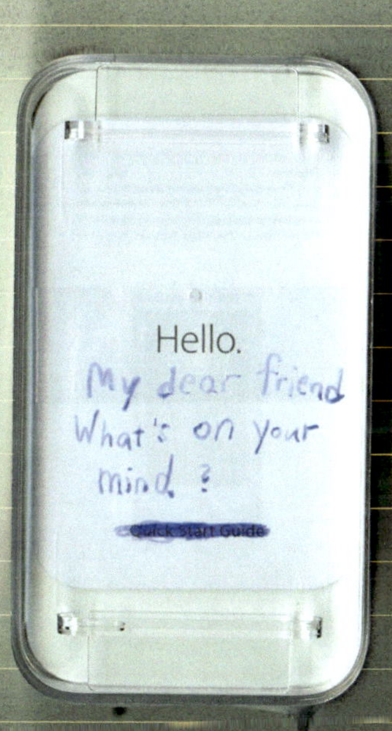
Hello.
My dear friend
What's on your
mind ?
Quick Start Guide

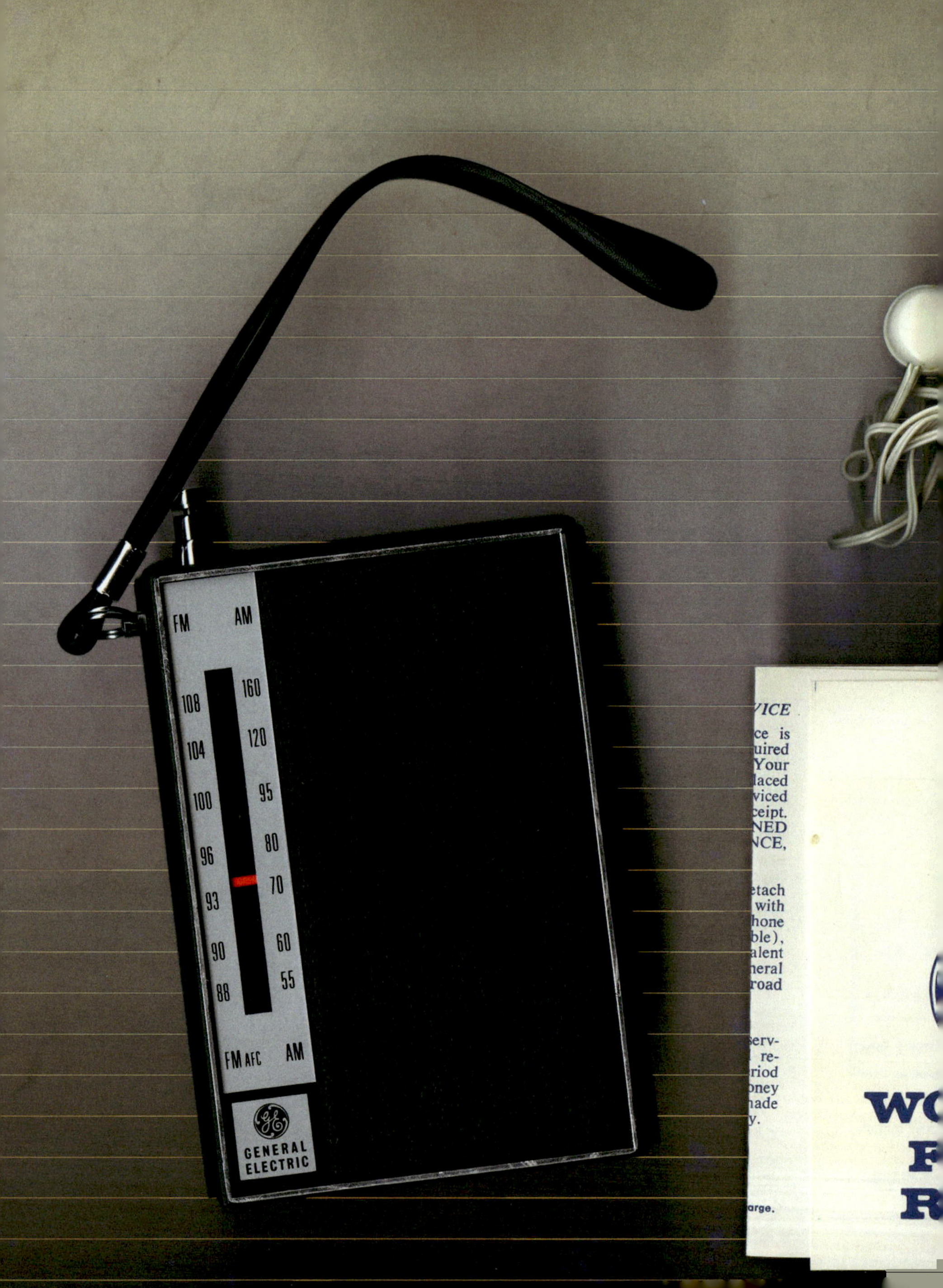

FM   AM
108   160
104   120
100   95
96   80
93   70
90   60
88   55
FM AFC   AM
GENERAL
ELECTRIC

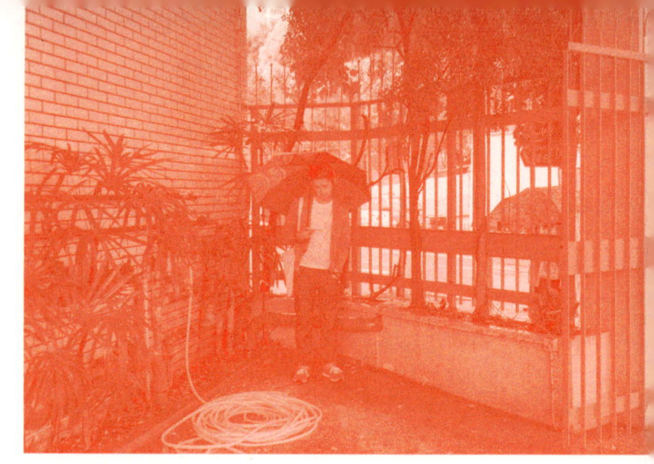

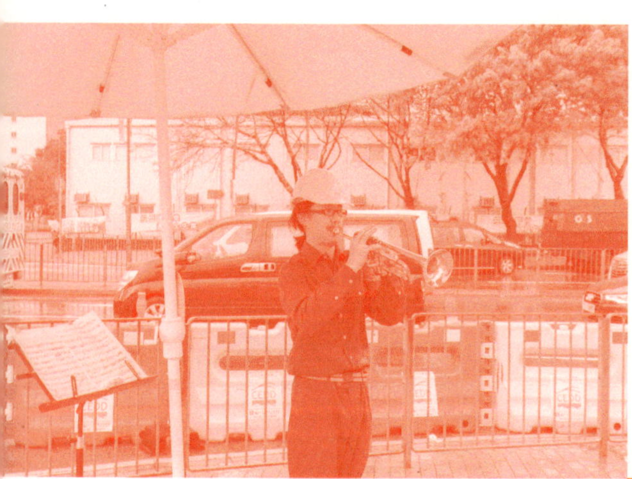

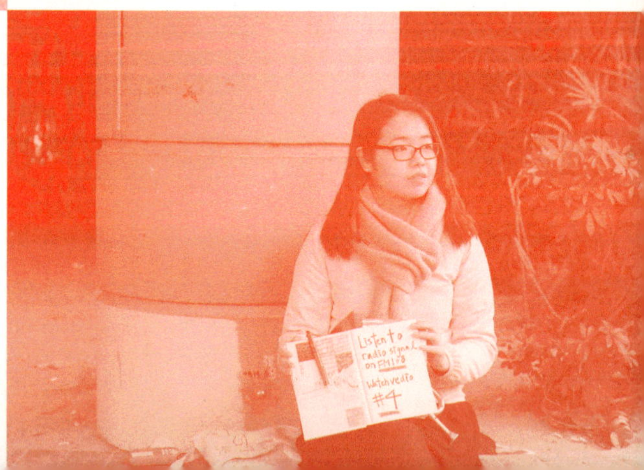

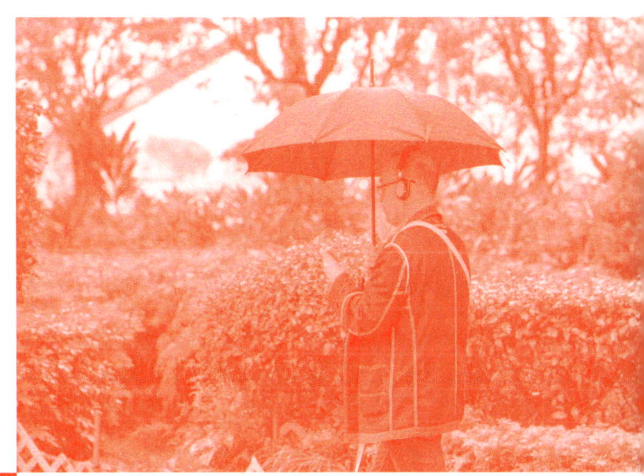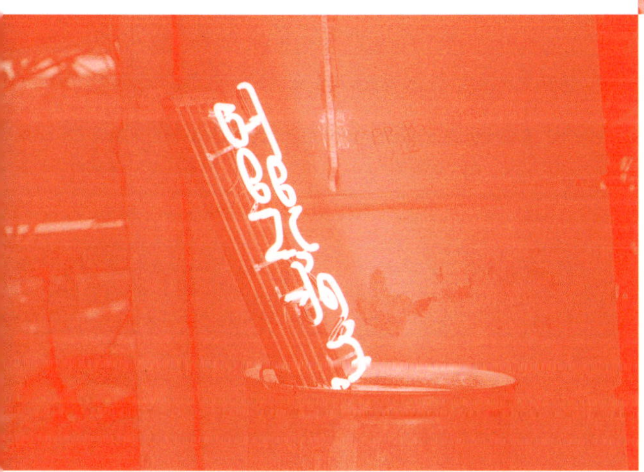

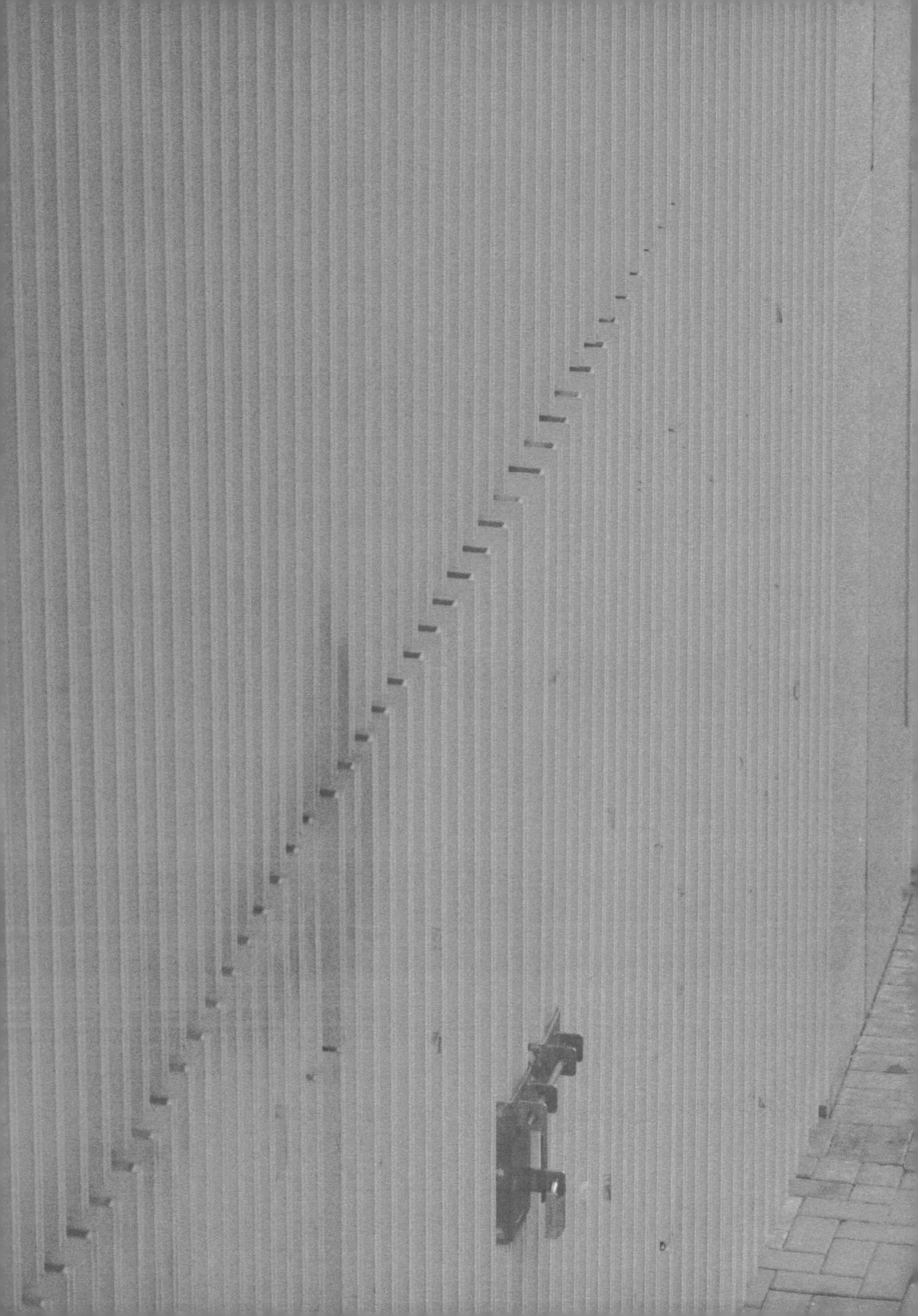

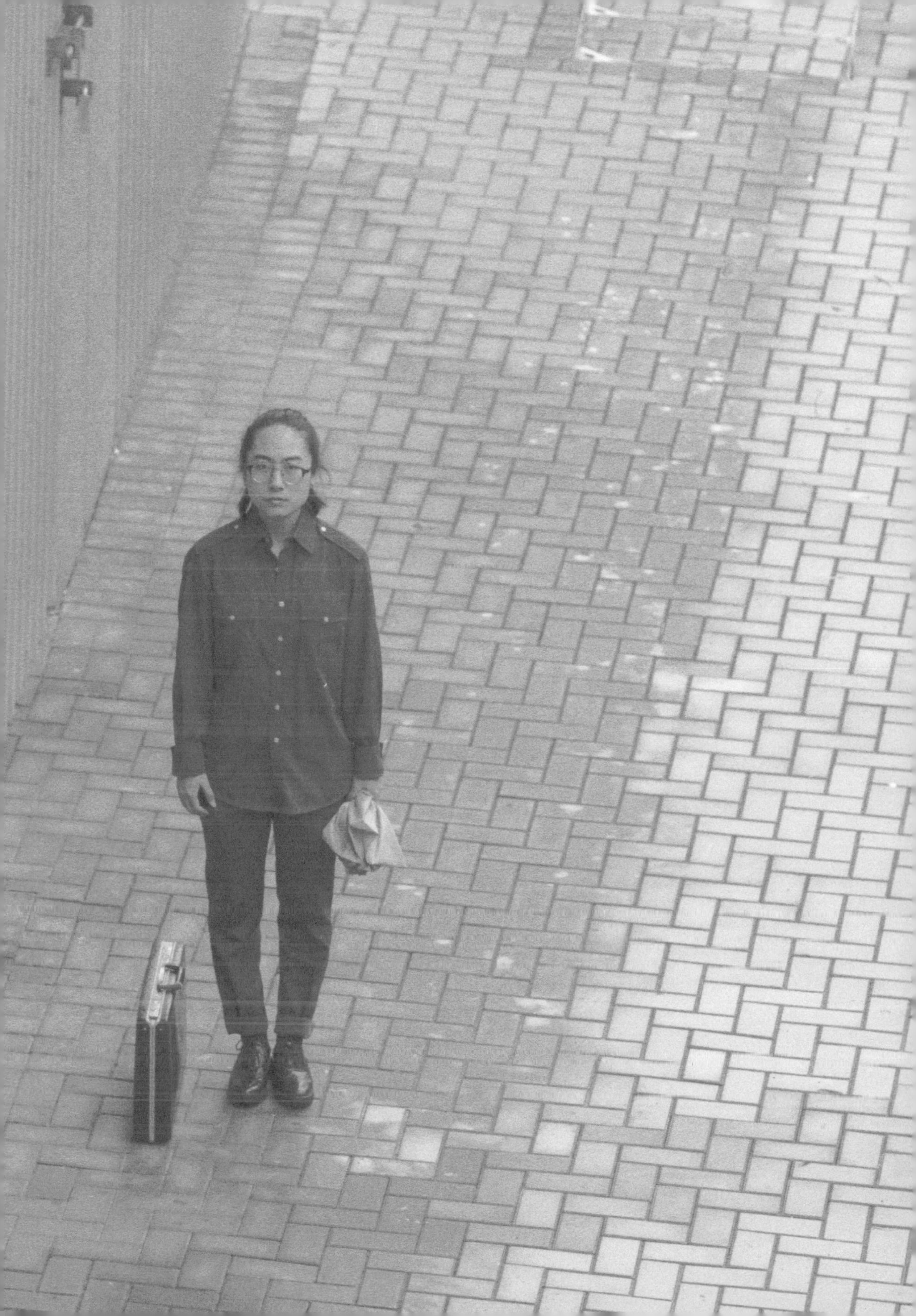

These Bells Have Changed Me in Fundamental Ways

Samson Young in Conversation with András Szántó

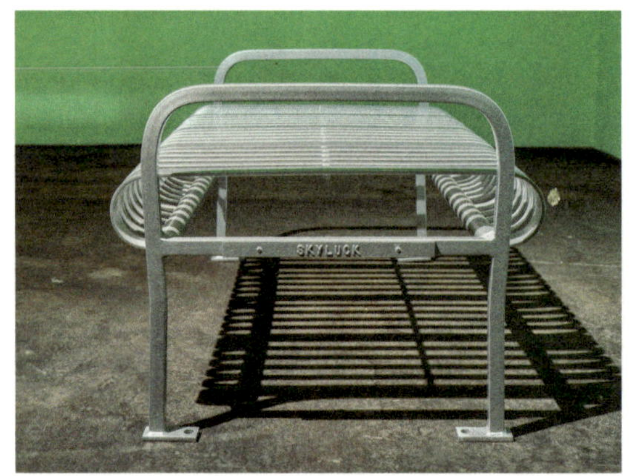

We are speaking now in May of 2016, about a half-year after you completed the BMW Art Journey. I think it is very interesting that the first major work you are doing since the journey deals with human migration. Do you think that to some extent this idea of movement was on your mind as you were traveling last year?

I often like to turn to topics in my work that in real life are violent or problematic, and I try to turn these into something that can occasion beauty. How do you arrive at a nuanced position on something as complicated as migration and human movement? I am not trying to sway opinion. I am looking inward. Through making the work and digging through history, both personal and institutional, I hope to arrive at a considered response to a very complex issue.

So what exactly did you conceive for Art Basel this June?

There is a sound cannon that police use to disperse protesters. It is called LRAD, which stands for Long Range Acoustic Device. It is basically a sonic weapon. I have been looking into getting my hands on one. I called up the distributor in Beijing. They were very suspicious of our motives at first, and so we lied and said we needed it for an outdoor music festival. They kept telling us that only the police or military would need them, and wouldn't sell it to us. So I emailed my gallerist Regina, in Cologne, and she called up the German distributor and told them that we would use it for an artwork. They had no problem selling it to us—which I find slightly disturbing.

So I am using one of these to beam birdsongs from one end of the space to the other end. I will be elevated on a perch about six meters off the floor. The audience will hear the birdsongs at about one hundred meters from me. They will also be elevated from the show floor at the listening positions. I am making some drawings of birdsongs, but only songs of birds considered to be of "the least concern" in terms of being endangered, or birds that are commonly considered to be pests—they make beautiful songs regardless of our opinion of them.

How does this connect to migration and the movement and displacement of people across borders?

The work leaps from one idea to another, but the bird is the metaphor that ties everything together. The LRAD actually uses the same technology that is used to repel "pest birds" on private properties, such as airport runways and nuclear-power facilities. I started thinking about the songs of birds that we do not want, and also about how birds learn their songs—by imitation.

Another point of reference has been the Vietnamese refugee crisis in Hong Kong. I found a news article, published on 6 July 1979, which happens to be the day I was born, about a freighter called *Skyluck* that carried 3,466 Vietnamese refugees. The *Skyluck* incident was really the beginning of a refugee crisis in Hong Kong that lasted for two decades. When I was a kid, when you turned on the radio at night, there would be a Vietnamese broadcast. It was preceded with an announcement in Vietnamese about refugee management. At school, we would make fun of it (of course, there was nothing funny about it) by imitating the sounds of the broadcast. Even now, when Hong Kong people refer to this period, they imitate the first several Vietnamese characters from that radio broadcast. It had a melodic quality, even though it was about something quite severe.

My dad came to Hong Kong from China on a boat illegally when he was eleven. It is something we never talked about. It was not until now, as I was looking into this history of refugees in Hong Kong and interviewing them, that I started to remember that my father also went through something similar.

At the "broadcasting position" you will see me high up with an LRAD. When you get to the "listening position" at the other end of the hall, you will get a very nice elevated view of the fair. You will hear birdsongs, both pre-recorded songs and "bird call imitations" performed live by me, which will be played back via the LRAD. You will also see a water basin, which is a replica of a plastic basin that the Vietnamese refugees arriving in Hong Kong received when they were detained. They would use these basins to wash, to bathe, but also to eat. The basin is produced by a popular local brand. I got one of these, 3D-scanned and then printed it, and made it into a bird fountain.

Looking back at the journey, how did it turn out as you envisaged, and how did it turn out differently?

It was close to how I imagined it. We had worked out quite a bit of detail in advance. And more important, I didn't have a clear picture of how I was going to record the bells and collect the materials. So I was improvisational. It turned out to be about 80 percent as I had imagined.

Cologne was a bit frustrating. I really wanted to record the bells of the Cologne cathedral from the new mosque. On my first visit, I did some drawings up close, but I was not quite satisfied. The second time I went back, I tried to go to the mosque and record the bells from there. I couldn't get high enough. If you want to record a bell from far away, it is not about volume, but about being high enough. There is a TV tower next to the mosque; maybe it would have worked there, but I wasn't able to access it.

The Korean Bell of Friendship in Los Angeles posed a different problem. It rings only a few times a year, including on Constitution Day. I had the bad luck of showing up when they couldn't fund a community partner for the event, so there was no ringing. There were other tourists there who were equally disappointed. So I decided to capture the sound of a bunch of Korean tourists imitating the sound of the bells. They came and chanted, "Doooooooong." I thought that sound was even better.

Having spent a year so closely with bells, how do you now think about what they really mean for people?

I had read a lot about how bells can mean different things to people. I had some knowledge about what bells were known for. However, only after this journey

do I possess this knowledge in the real sense of the word. There are things you read in books, but not until you actually live through them do you really own that knowledge.

We are now talking to the Hong Kong Sinfonietta about a composition I will write for them for next year. This will be for orchestra and bells on tape. In Hong Kong, we do not hear bells so much anymore. It is hard to imagine how important bells still are to so many people all over the world. In Hong Kong, we do not have sonic room for bells. It is such a noisy city.

You have evolved some new ways of working during the journey and afterward. One was the art walk. How does it fit the arc of your evolution as an artist?

The initial idea wasn't to make a walk. As you remember, the plan for the Hong Kong performance last March was really messy at first. Then, after you gave me the idea to do this walk, I started to research the form and the topic that I am dealing with. The form —the sound walk—is something that had been done, and I had also done it myself in two other occasions, but not with such elaborate materials and planning. I later discovered that people in the theater world have done such walks too, which they called environmental theater.

When I first designed the walk, I only really had in mind a golden bell—the Admiralty area of Hong Kong is called "Golden Bell" in Chinese.

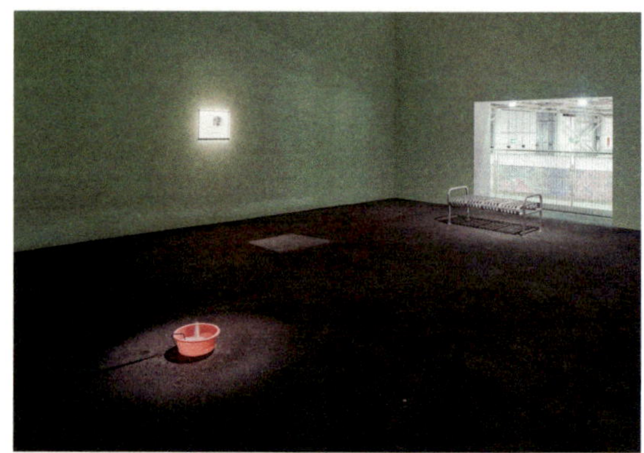

I started to look into the history of the district's curious Chinese name. Turns out that it has a connection with the military history of the place. I figured out that if I made the bell's original location the endpoint of the walk, then it would be just a fifteen-minute walk from the convention center —a perfect spot. So I decided to put the endpoint there—and in a way that decision really came out of a logistical concern.

When all of these details were laid out in front of me, the project started to become clearer. While this is not conscious, the endpoint of the sound walk—which is where the Golden Bell used to be located—is also the entrance to the occupy zones during the Umbrella Movement. Radio is another major point of reference in this walk, and my mother used to work in a factory that manufactured radios, back when there were still industries in Hong Kong.

The art walk participants entered into a kind of mythological space—full of Hong Kong tropes, but also a kind of personal mythology. What about those spooky spy characters?

In the walk, I constructed this world that is sort of semi-fictional, with family history, institutional records, and actual historic events all mixed in. I created this fictitious organization called the Ministry of Gentlemanly Warfare, which in the story is an underground organization of unidentified national origin that conducts forms of "sonic sabotage." Lok, the fictional protagonist of the story, is a senior engineering officer at the Radio Unit of the ministry. Lok uses the sounds of bells for the radio test signals, which he has been installing along the coast of Hong Kong under the organization's directives. This secret organization is loosely based on an actual organization that worked for Churchill during the Second World War.

It was gratifying to hear that you now believe both the bell project and the sound-walk project may continue to be part of your practice for years to come. You are still young. Where does the road lead from here?

I will definitely continue to make bell recordings. I think it will become a lifelong fascination. Just the other day, I discovered a little-known bell in Hong Kong that was left behind by the Americans during World War II, of which I plan to make a recording real soon.

I am in the habit of bringing my recording device wherever I go now, just in case I come across a significant bell.

As for the sound-walk format, I really enjoy how the form allows me to combine all of my interests (music composition, live performance, installation, drawings, narrative, voice acting, computer programming) into a site-specific experience. A few people had told me that my bell sound walk reminded them of Janet Cardiff's work at Documenta in 2013. I have not experienced that piece in person, but Cardiff is of course the most famous artist who is often associated with the format.

Yet there are actually many other lesser-known artists working in sound who've done excellent audio or video walks over the last two decades: UK-based Blast Theory's many audio and video walks; Lavinia Greenlaw's 2011 audio walk for a historic train station in Manchester; Waag Society & Esther Polak's 2003 Amsterdam PDA walk; the Livingverse Project in 2010 by Karl Baumann that shot iPod and iPad films on location; and Betsey Biggs's *11 Dreams in Red Hook* project in 2008—to name just a few. The walk has become such a popular format with sound artists that almost every sound artist I know has made at least one, but it is still something that is quite new to the contemporary art community. Before this most recent one, I'd actually already produced two walks, one in 2009, called *Urban Palimpsest*, and another in 2013, called *Your Very Empty Seat, or a Delicate Access*—the 2013 walk already had some videos and live performance elements in it. Both took place in Hong Kong.

In the fall of 2016, I will be making another audio-video walk for the nonprofit Project section at Frieze London, and in 2017 I will produce another one for the Manchester International Festival. The story of both of these new walks will be a kind of extension of the fictitious world that I created for the Art Basel Hong Kong one. You can think of them as sequels to the bell walk, and I will draw upon my bell sound archive again.

Whatever walks or travels come next, the BMW Art Journey is now over. It is clear that this was a very personal journey for you. What did you learn about yourself?

I think I would probably be dishonest if I told you I had an answer now. I think it will only come to me probably later. I don't think it has fully come to me yet.

One thing I did think about a lot—which I am still processing—is the danger of decontextualizing beauty to the effect of trivializing it.

We celebrate moments of beauty, often without a real sense of what it really means to live with them on a daily basis.

My journey concluded in Austria, and one of the last bells that I recorded was the Pummerin in Vienna, which produced waves of deep, voluminous vibration. How could anybody not find the Pummerin's sound beautiful, I thought? But then I was reminded of several court cases that I came across in my research, where residents living near bell towers attempted to put a stop to the regular tolling. So to paraphrase my own travelogue for the city of Vienna, I think there could be too much of a beautiful thing—sounds, even beautiful ones, have moments of aggression and do not care to be contained.

I was surprised by one of your emails, which had an almost confessional tone to it. It was a rumination on your identity, even your sexual identity. I remember thinking: *This is not about bells anymore.*

Yes, and it wasn't. I do think that these bells have changed me in fundamental ways I cannot yet fully articulate. It has something to do with being moral beings.

I was thinking a lot about this on my journey, because bells have been used in so many religious contexts. I just can't articulate it yet. I think the travelogue took on such a tone also because I was traveling alone most of the time during this research. I'd never traveled alone for such an extensive period of time. It encouraged me to look inward.

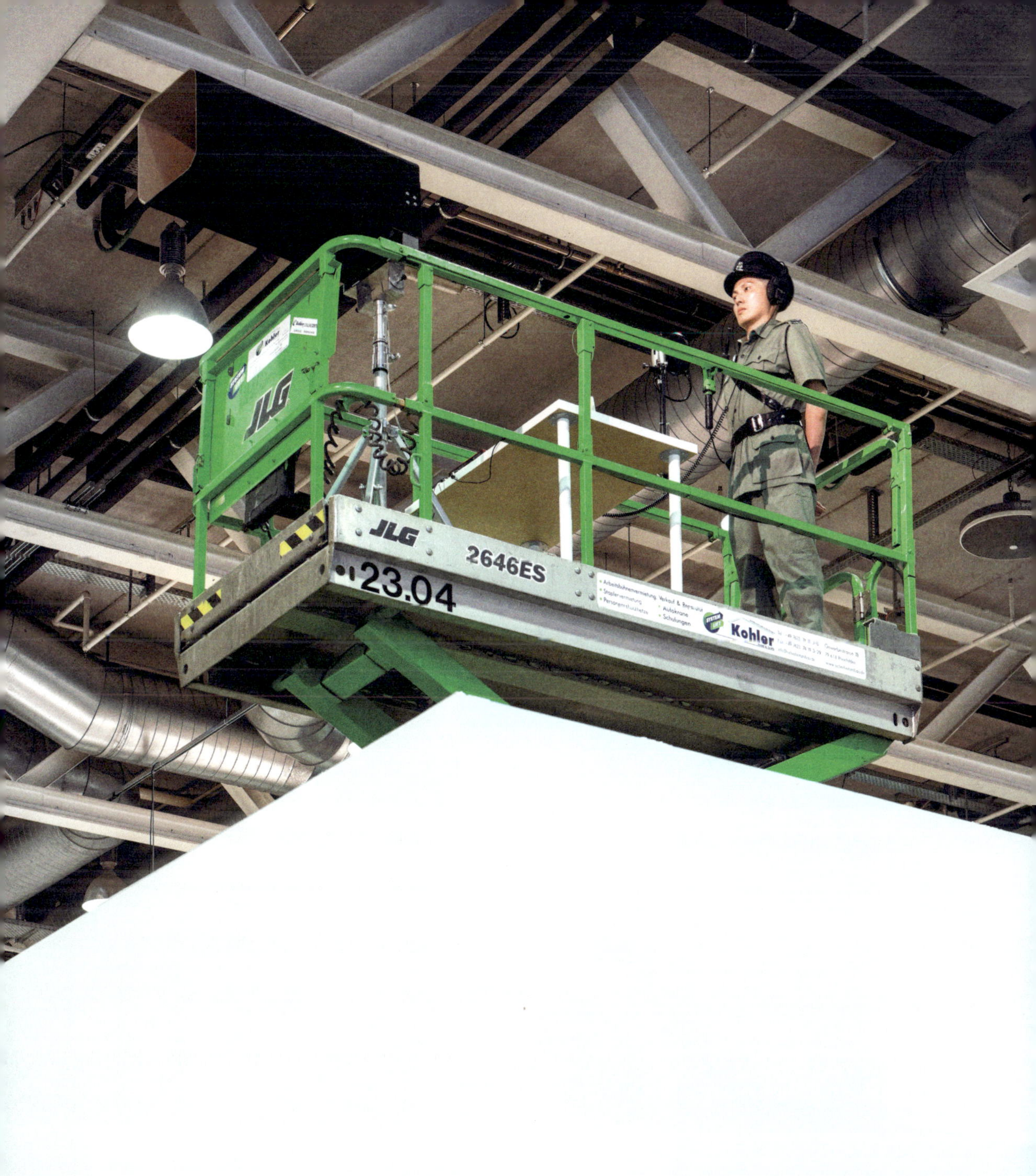

JLG
JLG 2646ES
23.04
Arbeitsbühnenvermietung Verkauf & Reparatur
Staplervermietung Autokrane
Personenschutz Schulungen
Kohler

List of illustrations

Editors
BMW Group, Munich
András Szántó

Managing Editor
Christiane Jekeli

Project Heads
Hedwig Solis Weinstein, BMW Group
Christiane Jekeli
Dorten studios, Berlin
Frauke Berchtig, Hatje Cantz

Contributors
Thomas Girst, Marc Spiegler,
András Szántó, Samson Young

Image Editor
Jacek Slaski

Copyeditor
Myles McDonnell

Graphic Design & Concept
Dorten studios, Berlin

Production
Julia Günther, Hatje Cantz

Printing, Binding, and Reproduction
DZA Druckerei zu Altenburg GmbH, Altenburg

Paper
Munken Print white 15, 115 g/m²;
Munken Print white 15, 150 g/m²;
Luxo Magic, 80 g/m²

© 2016
Hatje Cantz Verlag, Berlin,
and authors

Published by
Hatje Cantz Verlag GmbH
Mommsenstrasse 27
10629 Berlin
Germany
Tel. +49 30 3464678-00
Fax +49 30 3464678-29
www.hatjecantz.com
A Ganske Publishing Group company

Hatje Cantz books are available
internationally at selected
bookstores. For more information
about our distribution partners,
please visit our website at
www.hatjecantz.com.

Trade Edition
ISBN 978-3-7757-4170-5

Printed in Germany

Cover Illustration
Samson Young
DONG! (Mingun Bell, Myanmar), 2016
Watercolor, ink, crayon, stamp on paper
77.6 x 75 cm

About Samson Young

Selected Solo Exhibitions
2017: Hong Kong Pavillion, Venice Biennale. **2016:** Kunsthalle Düsseldorf, Germany. *The Mastery of Language Affords Remarkable Power,* Experimenter, Kolkata, India. *Orchestrations,* Connecting Space (presented by Para Site), Hong Kong. **2015:** *Pastoral Music,* Team Gallery, New York City. *Video Program: Samson Young,* Hiroshima City Museum of Contemporary Art, Japan. *Avant-garde on speed,* TKG+ gallery, Taipei. *Pastoral Music,* Discovery, Art Basel Hong Kong. **2014:** *I wanted to see everything: the Liquid Borders Project,* a.m. space, Hong Kong. **2013:** *On the Musically Beautiful,* Goethe-Institute, Hong Kong. **2011:** *Machines for Making Nothing,* Cogut Center for Humanities, Brown University, USA.

Selected Group Exhibitions
2016: *Retrogarde,* The Reva and David Logan Center for the Arts, University of Chicago. *CTRL+ALT,* Smithsonian Asian Pacific American Centre. *Canon,* Art Unlimited, Art Basel, Basel. **2015:** *48HR Incident,* 4A Centre for Contemporary Asian Art, Sydney. *Change Seed,* Center on Contemporary Art (CoCA), Seattle. *Kiinan Muuttuvat Maisemat,* Amos Anderson Museum, Helsinki, Finland **2014:** *Harmonious Society,* Asia Triennial Manchester 14, United Kingdom. *China's Changing Landscape,* Nordiska Akvarellmuseet, Sweden. *Journal of a Plague Year,* Arko Art Center, Seoul, South Korea. *A Time for Dreams - IV Moscow Biennale of Young Art,* Museum of Moscow. **2013:** *Revolution Per Minute: Sound Art China,* Shanghai West Bund Biennale of Architecture and Contemporary Art, Shanghai, China. *The Wizard's Chamber,* Kunsthalle Winterthur, Switzerland. *Innovationist: the Spectacular Journey of New Media Art,* Taipei Contemporary Art Museum, Taipei. **2012:** *Zero1 Biennial,* San Jose, California. *No Transnational: Liquid Borders and Empty Promises,* ISE Cultural Foundation, New York. **2011:** *XXX: Next Ten Years of Contemporary Art,* Today Art Museum, Beijing. *MONA FOMA,* Tasmania Museum and Art Gallery, Australia. **2010** *18 Degrees of Acclimation,* White Box Gallery, New York. **2009:** *Last Intervention,* Osage Gallery, Hong Kong. **2008:** *Dare to Struggle, Dare to Win: Emerging Artists from the Chinese Diaspora,* Deutsche Bank Headquarters, New York.

Selected Festival Presentations
2016: Internationale Ferienkurse für Neue Musik, Darmstadt, Germany. Fusebox Festival, Austin Texas. **2015:** New York Electronic Art Festival, Museum of Moving Images, New York. **2014:** Prix Cube 2014, Le Cube centre de creation numérique, Paris. Tonlagen Festival, Dresden, Germany. Transart Festival, Bolzano, Italy. INSTALAKCJE 3 - Festiwal Instalacji Muzycznych, Poland. **2013:** Lucerne Festival (Festival Lounge feat. the MIVOS Quartet), Switzerland. **2012:** Japan Media Art Festival, Tokyo, Japan. **2011:** MONA FOMA Festival of Music and Art, Australia. **2010:** Hong Kong Arts Festival. International Society of Contemporary Music (ISCM) Festival, Australia. **2008:** Canberra International Music Festival, Australia. Dark Music Days Contemporary Music Festival, Iceland. **2005:** Bang on a Can Summer Music Festival, Massachusetts Museum of Contemporary Art (MASS MoCA), USA.

Education
2013 Ph.D. in Music Composition, Princeton University.
2007: M.Phil. in Music Composition, University of Hong Kong.
2002: B.A. in Music, Philosophy and Gender Studies, University of Sydney.

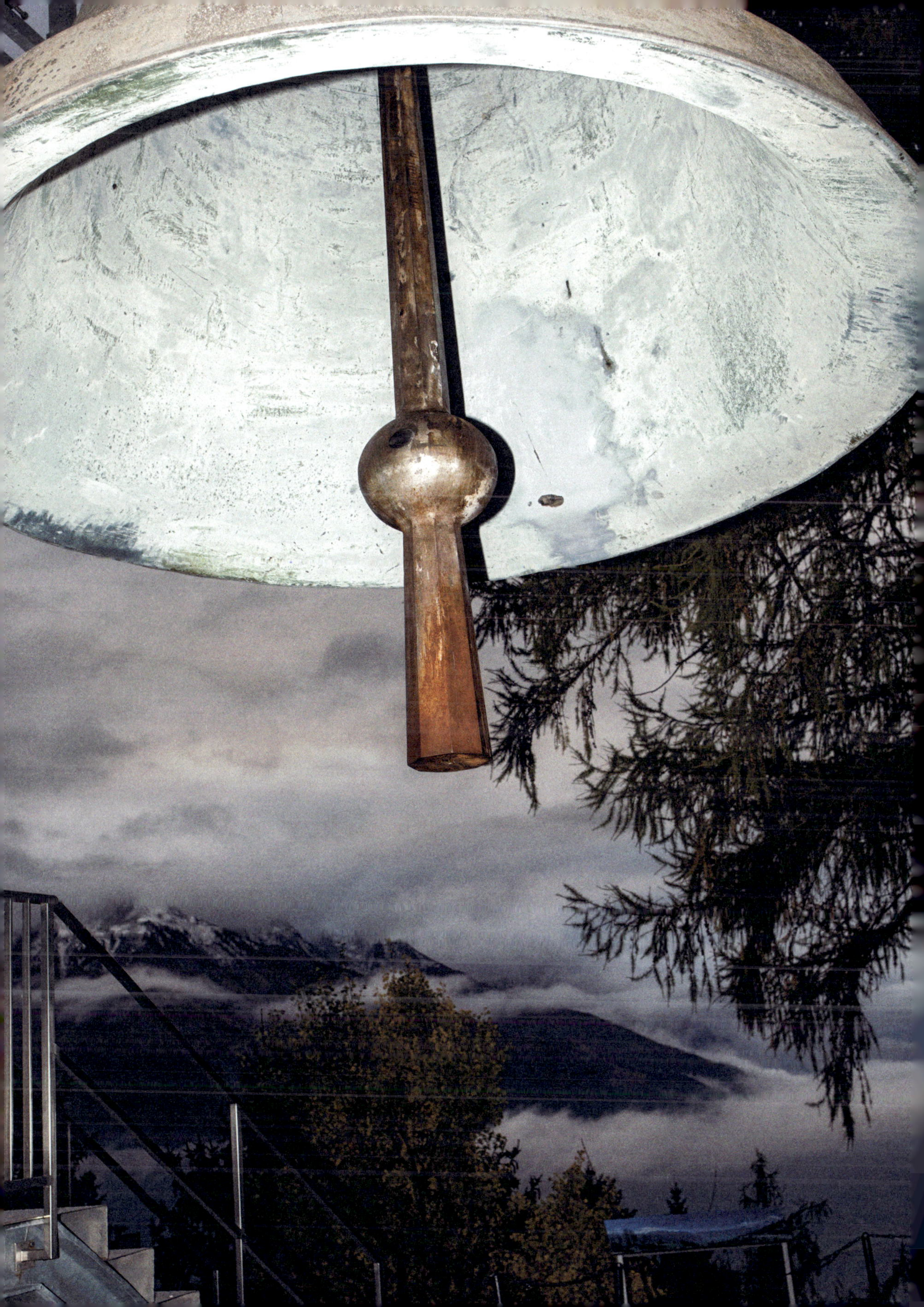

BMW ART JOURNEY

The BMW Art Journey is a joint initiative of Art Basel and BMW that offers artists an opportunity to undertake a journey of creative discovery to a destination of their own choosing. Like a mobile studio, the BMW Art Journey can take an artist to almost anywhere in the world—to establish contacts, to forge perspectives, to envision and create new work.

The BMW Art Journey is open to artists exhibited in the Discoveries sector of Art Basel in Hong Kong, and the Positions sector of Art Basel in Miami Beach.

In conjunction with the launch of the initiative, 2015 saw the publication of *The Sense of Movement: When Artists Travel* (Hatje Cantz), with examples of works by traveling artists in the past as an opener to a series of publications documenting the travels and projects of the BMW Art Journey recipients. *For Whom the Bell Tolls: Samson Young's Art Journey* is the first book in this series.

Recipients as of 2016

S a m s o n Y o u n g
For Whom the Bell Tolls:
A Journey into the History of Conflict
(Art Basel Hong Kong 2015)

H e n n i n g F e h r a n d P h i l i p p R ü h r
The Art of Memory:
Dub Music and the CCTV Tower
(Art Basel Miami Beach, 2015)

A b i g a i l R e y n o l d s
The Ruins of Time:
Lost Libraries of the Silk Road
(Art Basel Hong Kong 2016)

Art | Basel